Ed's journey with Jesus effectively reveals God's heart for His children. His sincere, transparent heart will be a source of encouragement, comfort, and strength for many, as it was for me. I will be purchasing copies for friends and family. Our most gracious and merciful God truly is a rewarder of anyone who will just come to Him.

— KC, *The Woodlands, Texas*

Ed's story is a confession of the struggle in our journey when we don't understand what is happening in our lives, yet we look to the One who does. We all have unmet desires; we can choose to become embittered, or we can submit those desires to Him and continue to put our trust and hope in God. As He did with Ed, God will also walk with us through our pain and disappointment.

— Jeanette Brewster, *Mission Builders International*

Knowing Ed and his journey, I challenge you to read and reread his story along with the Bible verses he used as his basis for his growing faith, his prayer discipline, and his strength. He recounts his reliance on the Lord's leading constantly to Father God, His Word, and building his faith in Him through prayer. He tells how the Lord and His Word were always brightest when the world around him was darkest.

—Jim and Joy McGatlin, *Mission Builders International*

We all live our lives with a desire for calling and deep purpose. A true disciple of Christ constantly submits those desires to His higher call and trusts His plan. *My Father Journey* is a powerful, personal look at a life submitted to His heavenly Father's call. If you need encouragement and hope for a difficult time in your walk, or help to stand firm for a prodigal, this book is for you.

—Raymond Franklin, *Elder, The Crossing Church*

My Father Journey

My Father Journey

The Weight of Waiting in Hope

Edward Wandell

My Father Journey
Copyright © 2023 by Edward Wandell
All rights reserved.

Published in the United States of America by Credo House Publishers,
a division of Credo Communications LLC, Grand Rapids, Michigan
credohousepublishers.com

ISBN: 978-1-62586-267-9

Unless otherwise indicated, Scripture quotations are taken from the Holy Bible, New International Version®, NIV® Copyright © 1973, 1978, 1984, 2011 by Biblica, Inc.™ Used by permission of Zondervan. All rights reserved worldwide. www.zondervan.com The "NIV" and "New International Version" are trademarks registered in the United States Patent and Trademark office by Biblica, Inc.™

Scripture quotations marked (NASB) are taken from the New American Standard Bible®, Copyright © 1960, 1971, 1977, 1995, 2020 by The Lockman Foundation. Used by permission.

Scripture quotations marked (NASB1995) are taken from the New American Standard Bible®, Copyright © 1960, 1971, 1977, 1995 by The Lockman Foundation. Used by permission.

Scripture quotations marked (KJV) are taken from the King James Version (KJV): King James Version, public domain.

Scripture quotations marked (NKJV) are taken from the New King James Version®. Copyright © 1982 by Thomas Nelson. Used by permission. All rights reserved.

Scripture quotations marked (ESV) are taken from The Holy Bible. English Standard Version® (ESV), copyright © 2001 by Crossway, a publishing ministry of Good News Publishers. Used by permission. All rights reserved.

Scripture quotations marked (NLT) are taken from the Holy Bible, New Living Translation, copyright © 1996, 2004, 2015 by Tyndale House Foundation. Used by permission of Tyndale House Publishers, Inc., Carol Stream, Illinois 60188. All rights reserved.

Scripture quotations marked (AMP) are taken from the Amplified Bible, Copyright © 2015 by The Lockman Foundation. Used by permission.

Scripture quotations marked (BSB) are taken from The Holy Bible, Berean Study Bible, BSB. Copyright © 2016, 2018 by Bible Hub. Used by Permission. All Rights Reserved Worldwide.

Cover and interior design by Believe Book Design

Editing by Donna Huisjen

Printed in the United States of America
First Edition

Contents

Introduction 9

Chapter 1	What Is a Father Journey?	13
Chapter 2	"Write It Down"	19
Chapter 3	Starting the Journey	25
Chapter 4	Wait, This Is about Her, Isn't It?	31
Chapter 5	Burden—the Weight of Waiting in Hope	35
Chapter 6	"What If" Kind of Faith	41
Chapter 7	"Even If" Kind of Faith	45
Chapter 8	"No Matter What" Kind of Faith	57
Chapter 9	Suffering and Perseverance: All Kinds for a Little While	63
Chapter 10	Suffering and Character: Purposeful Pain	71
Chapter 11	Suffering and Hope: Unrequited love	79
Chapter 12	The Need to Have Need	83
Chapter 13	Isaiah 54 vs. a Plumbing Predicament	91
Chapter 14	Am I on a Roller Coaster?	95
Chapter 15	An Injustice, an Embrace, a Promise, and Encouragement	103
Chapter 16	Areas of Growth and My Path for Progress	109
Chapter 17	Hope and Healing	119
Chapter 18	Thoughts of My Ongoing Journey	129

Acknowledgments 135

Introduction

Most journeys conjure up appealing images of adventures that are anticipated, planned for, and then lived out. We design to be outside our normal confines and routines, experiencing new and tantalizing tastes, sights, and distractions from normal daily life.

Then there are journeys that start out with distressing news and the heaviness of a boat anchor. They pounce on us with the ferocity of a hungry lion and strike fear into our hearts.

My journey of a broken marriage relationship "looked" like the latter—it was not the trip I wanted to take. Sometimes decisions and directions are made for us just as this ticket for my journey was purchased for me. I was about to walk into the unwelcome fog of the unknown.

Slowly, as the initial fire of hurt and confusion diminished, the remaining ashes miraculously retained an ember of hope. God, waiting for me to invite Him into my troubles, asked me to stand for His best while trusting Him in the thick of my gloom without knowing what may lay ahead for me.

It became self-evident that in my hope and trust I had some choices to make to show God that my hope was genuine, and my trust was true. To ask Him for grace and favor with little commitment on my part would not be a good start to my journey.

With little surprise, it turns out there are many choices each of us need to consider to get into stride with our heavenly Father—to start looking at things from His viewpoint. Some of these are easier than others but all lay the groundwork and pattern of obedience in our trust.

Soon enough are the very sobering choices that are mercifully discovered along the way of our journey only after we have been built-up and strengthened by the Lord because of His trust in us. Even if our cause is righteous and we are steadfast we will be faced with battles that test our decisions beyond what we had imagined.

There will be an internal battle when our road forks to offer either a luring promise of a thousand painless pleasures or an uncertain path of ten thousand tears, or another fork leading back to the known and complacent acceptance of life's current, but difficult circumstances or a new and faith-filled journey of profitable growth and healing. We will be tested to choose either a journey of self, or a journey of the Father.

I got to decide how I would respond to what was being visited upon me by the choices I made. What was I going to do at this juncture in my life? Choose the easier and acceptable way of terminating a marriage of someone I loved, or listen to God and follow a very uncertain and difficult path He wanted me to take?

In the uninvited journey that lay in front of you is a fork. What path do you choose?

Fortunately, we are not on this journey by ourselves. In fact, I didn't really choose my path—my Father chose me. However, I did listen and chose to take the first step of this, My Father Journey. He made the right choice and so did I, for man's plans are temporal, God's plans and blessings are eternal.

Journey with me to see how my hope grew into improbable joy, my patience matured in my afflictions, and my faithfulness fanned into flames in my prayers. My fog lifted to reveal greater purposes for me. God had purpose to instill into me a trust of Him for much greater things "no matter what."

God also has purpose for me to grab someone's hand and walk along with them on their Father journey. To help you pursue your purpose, the goal of this book is to:

- Share with you the hope that has been birthed in me from my journey. "Searchers" (those who are looking for God's purpose in the pain they are experiencing) will relate greatly to the transparent, plain, and raw emotions I share about my struggles.

- Then fan the flames of your hope and encouragement.
- Become a catalyst for you to grow your own faith that gets Gods attention while becoming a channel for His promises.
- Encourage a hunger for God's deep and healing grace—a well of immeasurable depth.

Travel a path with me to discover what our Creator has purposed for you whether you are surrounded by the fog and gloom of life or facing a difficult fork in your road.

"And after you have done everything, to stand" (Ephesians 6:13).

Chapter 1

What Is a Father Journey?

*He is making all things new. He is working all things out.
Maybe not according to my plan, but by a good, good plan.
He sees the whole; I see the small.*

This book is a story of a journey. Not a planned-out, I-know-where-this-is-headed kind of trip, but a full-fledged, no map, plunging headlong into the valleys, gasping up to the mountaintops, storm-filled, tear-drenched, drought-ravaged, broken compass, seemingly never-ending, not knowing odyssey. Had I known of all this upcoming "fun," I might have opted out and taken a U-turn while still in my valley many years ago.

I had simply asked God to heal a broken marriage relationship, and this is what He said to me: "Come, follow me." Sure, why not? I assumed that following God would likely involve a couple of lonely weeks, a few pride-testing apologies, heartfelt tears, several counseling sessions, and some earnest prayers. I would put my hand back in hers and we'd give it another go. NOT! I wasn't quite that naïve, but neither was I prepared for what God had in mind.

I met with God many times. I wanted to help Him plan this "trip" we were taking. Often, I cried, offering solutions while pointing at my watch, suggesting some timelines that made some sense to me for this reunion. With much patience, God slowly started to prepare my heart for my upcoming journey: be still, trust Him, and He will fight for me. Yeah, right. I had too many good ideas and willingness to share them to be benched!

Without a doubt I believed that God was just as eager to restore my marriage as I was. His starting point, however, I wrestled with.

He drew me closer and began to teach me some spiritual principles and truths that reflect His very character, who He is, and who I am. I learned that this is important because His character is the foundation of His purpose for me and the roadmap to get me there. I soon realized that His path would deepen our relationship as I discovered and learned to trust in His very deep care for me.

Along the way, He also started to give me opportunities to put into practice His plan for my new growth. Very soon, I found His teaching and the practical homework He assigned were humbling and unnatural to me. His trust-building training sessions were well beyond the typical Sunday school Bible lessons I had encountered. With exercise, my trust in Him grew, allowing for more revelation and training for new growth. I learned that this is relationship building God's way.

My major assignment—God wanted me to learn to identify with and live my life more like the father's. What father? A must starting point for us is reading the prodigal son story from the Bible in Luke 15:11–32.

The Parable of the Prodigal Son

Jesus continued: "There was a man who had two sons. The younger one said to his father, 'Father, give me my share of the estate.' So he divided his property between them.

"Not long after that, the younger son got together all he had, set off for a distant country and there squandered his wealth in wild living. After he had spent everything, there was a severe famine in that whole country, and he began to be in need. So he went and hired himself out to a citizen of that country, who sent him to his fields to feed pigs. He longed to fill his stomach with the pods that the pigs were eating, but no one gave him anything.

"When he came to his senses, he said, 'How many of my father's hired servants have food to spare, and here I am starving to death! I will set out and go back to my father and say to him: Father, I have sinned against heaven and against you. I am no longer worthy to be called your son; make me like one of your hired servants.' So he got up and went to his father.

"But while he was still a long way off, his father saw him and was filled with compassion for him; he ran to his son, threw his arms around him, and kissed him.

"The son said to him, 'Father, I have sinned against heaven and against you. I am no longer worthy to be called your son.'

"But the father said to his servants, 'Quick! Bring the best robe and put it on him. Put a ring on his finger and sandals on his feet. Bring the fattened calf and kill it. Let's have a feast and celebrate. For this son of mine was dead and is alive again; he was lost and is found.' So they began to celebrate.

"Meanwhile, the older son was in the field. When he came near the house, he heard music and dancing. So he called one of the servants and asked him what was going on.

'Your brother has come,' he replied, 'and your father has killed the fattened calf because he has him back safe and sound.'

"The older brother became angry and refused to go in. So his father went out and pleaded with him. But he answered his father, 'Look! All these years I've been slaving for you and never disobeyed your orders. Yet you never gave me even a young goat so I could celebrate with my friends. But when this son of yours who has squandered your property with prostitutes comes home, you kill the fattened calf for him!'

"'My son,' the father said, 'you are always with me, and everything I have is yours. But we had to celebrate and be glad, because this brother of yours was dead and is alive again; he was lost and is found.'"

My assignment and story began with me calling out to God in pain and in desperate need. Of course, I didn't imagine that my pain and need were both largely self-centered and nearsighted. This realization came slowly to me. Through the voice of His Holy Spirit, speaking from a realm only God speaks from, I began to recognize it as not my own mind speaking but His. He reframed the picture, teaching me how my path forward related to this parable. Through my thoughts, inclinations, Bible studies, questions, and the wrestling of my heart's desires, His voice was getting through to my mind and heart. Because I had a need, I was listening as never before.

I had read the prodigal son parable numerous times through the years, and I didn't think there was much more there for me. I would always come away with the same impression that it was about the younger son. After all, its title references him. The parable is indeed about the younger son, who had made some selfish and foolish mistakes and, in the end with a changed heart, wanted to return to his father and the provision and security of home and family. There would be a rare reader of this parable who would not be able to identify with him on some level, even if their actions hadn't included leaving home. A wayward youth comes home wiser. A noble message.

But then we have the older brother. He seems to be a supporting actor to add both another moralizing lesson and some familial dysfunctional appeal. Most of us will view him through a window whereby we can still watch his bad behavior, yet shield ourselves from the obvious infectious, COVID-19-like nature of such attitudes in our own hearts. We smugly say to ourselves, and to anyone else who will listen, that at least we aren't as self-centered as he is. However, with a more honest introspection, we all come to the same conclusion—the window is really a mirror.

The father? He was just one of those idealistic, Hallmark kind of dads I could not relate to. He was a strawman in the story to help put a bow on the ending of a good moral tale—be appreciative of what you have and don't run away. Maybe someone won't shame you and will welcome you back if you do mess things up.

Reread the story. The father *is* the story, and we all are the supporting actors. He is an embodiment, a human picture of the heart and character of God Himself. In telling this parable, Jesus is sharing His Father's character as He teaches us how to experience and extend the same love, joy, and longsuffering faithfulness that the prodigal's father demonstrated.

My journey was given life by my wife, who left our home and marriage. She became my prodigal, looking for new life on her terms, which then caused this nice, fuzzy, but formerly not very relevant Bible parable to smack me in the face. God's patient leading and encouragement aroused me to fight for and to stand for my marriage even long after the judge's ink had dried on the divorce decree. I've become a "stander"—someone who is fighting for a covenant marriage relationship that God has desire and purpose to restore.

God is maturing the very imperfect me so that, when my promised one comes home, He will add two healed souls together to make a healthy whole. This maturation process, or journey, that God has me on is to make me more Father-like, putting on love, which binds everything together in perfect harmony.

> *And above all these put on love, which binds everything together in perfect harmony.*
>
> Colossians 3:14 (ESV)

Now you know why this book is titled *My Father Journey*.

I believe the lessons I am learning are not only for prodigal children or fractured relationships but are reflections of God's heart for all to learn. He desires each of us to work through some deep and hard truths, while building a relationship with Him to carry out His eternal purposes by helping us build Father-like relationships with others.

All this over a divorce? Yeah, I've heard that before. "Let her go, there are better women out there. Why would you want to pursue someone who has hurt you so?" Thankfully, God got to me before the negative Nancys did. He lit the fire. He grabbed my heart before I went charging back out into the world with a wounded soul and a very impaired faith. This was God's doing. I was unsure why I was listening or willing to obey until I understood this Scripture:

> *Dear friends, you always followed my instructions when I was with you. And now that I am away, it is even more important. Work hard to show the results of your salvation, obeying God with deep reverence and fear.*
>
> *For God is working in you, giving you the desire and the power to do what pleases him.*
>
> Philippians 2:12–13 (NLT)

Paul reminds us that God is providing the want-to and the ability for us to grow our faith. It cannot be created or sustained by the faith of others but must be personally rooted and empowered by Him alone.

Chapter 2

"Write It Down"

On my 65th birthday I awoke wide-eyed at 3:30 a.m. to another unexpected assignment! God dropped a fully surprising thought into my spirit: "Ed, you've experienced a lot, and I want you to write this stuff down." And He gave me this title: "My Father Journey." I didn't know why or who or what this assignment was for. Was it going to be a devotional? A book? (I had never even thought about writing a book.) Very possibly, He was keeping me positively engaged and growing while He was at work. At the very least, I knew this was going to be for me. Putting my thoughts on paper has always helped me to process my feelings.

I also know that God wants to use our testimony and our individual experiences where we have seen Him orchestrating our lives, other people's situations, events, and time. I am praying that the truths and lived reality of my story will help to encourage others to search for healing and a deeper relationship with Jesus and with others.

Having been on a stormy ride for many years, I knew that I was on a journey because I was nowhere near the place where I had last experienced any normalcy and sanity, and I had no idea where I was headed. I was stumbling around searching for God, as well as for some meaningful purpose in all my mess since my prodigal's departure. I was also determinedly searching for a specific destination and outcome—her return and our restoration.

Though I wasn't the one who had set the waves in motion by leaving our marriage, this had become an opportunity for God to speak faith and direction into my life, squeezing as much redemptive purpose out of this trial as possible. My journey had already been far too long and painful and full of "stuff" to be anything but a place for God to show up and do some redeeming.

Not knowing where this all ends does little to change my direction or purpose but does much in terms of how I respond to it. Without a doubt this story is ultimately about God's love in each of our lives and His desire for our trust in all things.

First Corinthians 13:12 (ESV) says:

> *For now we see in a mirror dimly, but then face to face. Now I know in part; then I shall know fully, even as I have been fully known.*

This passage opened my eyes to the truth that I can search out and pray for wisdom and earnestly try to make sense of my circumstances, though I am seeing things only dimly. God knows the whys, the hows, and the whens. I'm learning to trust in that.

I was practicing doing what I heard God saying. It was easy to be a selective hearer when I first started listening for Him: "That wasn't really Him, was it?" "I can't see that working out." "He didn't really say that, did He?" I had a choice: listen to what I believed was His voice . . . or not listen.

Around this time, I heard a message from Isaiah 30. The central point was to obey first and look back and understand later. I decided to start writing. Just as in my already underway "standing" journey, if I had known all the twists and turns of writing about it, I probably would not have listened so carefully.

I don't like reliving intense emotions and trying at the same time to commit coherent thoughts to a screen. This is very time consuming and draining. It would be easier to chalk it all up to experience and move on. I have prayed many times to God to allow me to do just that. That did not work out. He left me in this for a reason.

When I pray Psalm 139:23–24, I want to look past my feelings and see underneath what God sees, like a check of my spirit:

> *Search me, God, and know my heart; test me and know my anxious thoughts.*
>
> *See if there is any offensive way in me, and lead me in the way everlasting.*

I use God's Word to divide truth and feelings because I can spend too much time and get sidetracked focusing on my own thoughts. I don't want to be deceived, but, rather, through an intimacy with Jesus, I long to be taught of His better way, His truth.

While my searching takes me to places high and low, under the rocks, on top of the mountains, down into the valleys, and into places I have not looked before, my desire is to find the voice and heart of God. Some searches are productive, and some are not (you will probably deduce that from the jumbled route I take!).

My writing is not all original but is a tidied-up collection of thoughts from my personal journals and study and sermon notes from past years (I recognize and thank all the preachers and teachers who have been faithful to God's leading). As a hungry Christian, humbled and healing from my own brokenness and prodigal days, I regularly review and ponder this trove of wisdom, refreshing myself with truth along my path. Reminding myself corrects my course and affirms to me that I am making progress. These treasures became a fount for my journey and a source of inspiration for this book.

This is not meant to be a "how-to" book, though in my excitement and conviction it may sometimes seem to be a bit sermon-like. There are many things I don't understand enough to even begin to tell another person how to walk their path, but I am hoping the reader will glean enough to apply to his or her own journey. There will also be things you will learn not to do. But this is my journey—as messy as it is.

You may be in a similar spouse or child prodigal situation. If you do not feel led to become a "stander," do not let my zealousness bring you any guilt. Follow where God is leading you. This isn't a race. You don't need to fully buy in to this standing thing all at once.

Certainly, I think it paramount for each person to seek out the wisdom of God for their own individual path—my path won't look like your path, and my spiritual meat might be your milk. I pray my story will have some helpful and encouraging touch points for you. Why encouraging? Because when you are neck deep in life's problems, it is natural to feel alone and hopeless, without seeing a path forward. When someone comes along and puts words and feelings to your issues, your hope meter moves up a bit. When your fog of confusion and hopelessness has a spotlight shone on it by someone else who has walked in a similar dark wilderness, your heart starts beating to a different tune. My story will bless you as my hearing about God's work in your life would bless me.

I'm neither a writer nor a pastor. I am not theologically trained and don't consider myself a teacher. You may find some of my thoughts, views, and beliefs erroneous, as I also may after a few years of further wrestling with them. This is a chronicle of my journey. The result of our reaching for God's calling in our life will always be one of learning.

As you read, remember our friend Job's appeal:

> *"Do you intend to rebuke my words, when the words of one in despair belong to the wind?"*
>
> Job 6:26 (NASB)

I don't think all my words belong to the wind, but some might! Some of my tenses might flip and seem confusing. I have and I am still experiencing many things. No question, I feel confused at times!

One of the great aspects about God is how He treats each one of us as individuals. Your fighting skills are sharpened in your own battles and in your own trenches, muddied by your own tears. It could be ugly, messy, and frustrating. In our pressing battles God is making new wine, a renewed love and intimacy with God made ready for harvest. The fruit is a closer walk with Him, resulting in a deep and daily source of joy.

God made our hands for battle and our fingers for war, and He wants to make each of us a conquering warrior, not a child with an imaginary sword. He wants us to be a battleship, not a rowboat. We learn to fight by fighting, and we are not conquerors unless we beat something up. Our battles are opportunities to become conquerors for the kingdom of God.

My writing identifies numerous Scriptures that have counseled and encouraged me, but many more are imbedded in the narrative. Make no mistake, though: God's Word, His written revelation to His creation, has been my constant lifeboat, my hiding place, and the light on my path the whole time. It has been and continues to be my only hope.

I invite you to read my chronicle of this journey and learn why and how God is teaching me not to resent but to embrace what He has given me.

Chapter 3

Starting the Journey

For how do you know, O wife, whether you will save your huband? Or how do you know, O husband, whether you will save your wife?

1 Corinthians 7:16 (NKJV)

As of this writing, my wife left our home over four years ago. Though, certainly, my journey started long before this one event.

Many years ago in my first marriage, I too had left for the "far country." I sought after and received a divorce. Though there were plenty of hurts that had grown between us, unloving actions and responses from both of us, I carry the guilt and shame for having been the one who retreated into sin, called it quits, and left the marriage. This was a very painful and humbling period for me as a Christ follower.

I can't imagine the pain that I caused and the ripples that still emanate from that decision. I knew it was a selfish act, but I felt very desperate, lonely, and unloved during a long struggle with depression. This was a very sobering experience that left me grasping for the pieces of my life that had been left strewn about my pigsty.

Somehow, in this terrible muck, God watered the seed of human value through His grace. Since I was very low and no longer had any pretenses to hide behind, that seed germinated in me from a broken spirit and contriteness, with a lot of good muck for fertilizer. I was able only to look up and was given the grace to know that this experience would not define who I was. Thus started an immediate, deeper, and more earnest search for God's healing in my life.

True repentance, forgiveness—given and received, Bible study, prayer, transparency in men's groups, fellowship with believers, life-giving worship, and solid preaching led me on a path to a better understanding and experience of the breadth and depth of God's grace and mercy. I started to deeply inhale into my wounded soul for the first time the character of God and to see how He was working for me and leading me to a freedom from the guilt and shame I had lived with. He cared too much for me to leave me in a wounded and apathetic condition. He saw potential in me.

I was beginning to understand and experience the reason for the trials He had allowed in my life and how He was directing my paths. *Everything* God was doing or allowing in my life was for my good. This was not just the stuff of a good devotional; it was divine heart surgery!

> "My Father is always working, and so am I."
> John 5:17 (NLT)

I had experienced the plight of a prodigal firsthand. I had been chased by the Holy Spirit when I was running away, and it was not a good feeling, as my pride and self-sufficiency started to crumble. I knew the hurt of trying to flee, and I wasn't going to repeat some of my mistakes.

Several years after my first divorce, I met a beautiful, caring woman whom I grew to love deeply. We were married with the hope that our collective wisdom would help steer us away from our pasts. The details are unimportant here, but too soon we experienced turbulence in our marriage. At first I was quite reactive and defensive to the unfortunate unfolding events. The confusion and pain that were coming to the surface seemed surreal at times. I struggled anxiously to hold on.

My bewildered and searching heart only drove me on a deeper quest for God. I ran again to where I had recently experienced affirmation and encouragement. He was waiting. He promises us that, if we search for Him, we will find Him.

> "You will seek me and find me when you seek me with all your heart."
> Jeremiah 29:13

A life lesson: We don't get to control what someone else wants to do. This is a hard, unforgiving, and ongoing lesson to be learned. But

I got a really fast introduction to it when she walked out of the house without a word. She was gone. Admittedly, there was some pride in me, some feelings of injustice, some denial, and some naive hope that she would turn around and say, "I'm sorry." Instead, I suffered shell shock!

It was the realization that I could do nothing in my own power to bring her back, and the anguish of facing another soul shaking, that pushed me into an even deeper hunt for God. He had been faithful last time; my eyes would again be riveted on Him!

I could have easily comforted myself in old sins and turned away to my own feelings, but I instead chose to run after Him. Why did I do this, when another tidal wave of strife had come barging into my life? This is of overriding importance when one is wanting to stop the pain and hopelessness of a very real struggle (either self-imposed or interposed from the outside). When we are hurting and confused, wrong thinking patterns can easily surface that lead us away from the very help being sought. I needed to learn godly thinking patterns for my life.

My searching heart and prayers were looking around every corner, and it soon became a common theme of the Holy Spirit to stir in me the thought that I could fight for my marriage and the woman I loved. After all, we had proclaimed together that "My lover is mine and I am hers" (Song of Solomon 2:16). We had too much that was right together to walk away from each other. I didn't know what this fight would look like, but everything I had been doing had left me feeling ineffective.

My pastor's counsel echoed in my head: "You both are wounded. Hurt people hurt people," so I knew God's will was for each of us to be whole and in right relationship with Him if we were to restore our marriage. This provided me a solid starting place to set my feet. Also, my right orientation toward God allowed Him to grow my trust in Him to wage this war—a war that I knew would be fought on my knees.

While this still smacked of some passivity, I knew I was in over my head. Because I saw the size of the giant in front of me, I slowly picked up my shield and unsheathed my sword. Encouragement from a God bigger than myself was being birthed in me to become a "stander"—standing for our relationship against our separation and praying against divorce.

I felt like cannon fodder in my battle when another bomb exploded in my face—divorce. Ouch! This wasn't supposed to go this way.

This. Really. Hurt. I cried many a river. My knees were sore. A divorce had such a sound of finality to it. I didn't want to cross this Rubicon. It would be over after this. It couldn't be reassembled. It was beyond God's help.

> All I could do was cry and ask, "Who took my loving wife?"

As the smoke cleared, the reality was a bit more extraordinary. Nothing changed in God's daily encouragement. Nothing changed in my walk and prayers. A truth sprouted in me: God is bigger than divorce! It became evident that this wasn't even a speed bump to Him.

My heart was still soft and searching for God's healing and restoration, while my resolve and hope only grew. The fact was, I loved my wife with an agape love described in 1 Corinthians 13. My motives and mission had not changed. I realized that my prayers were not passive, that God was engaged, and that the enemy was enraged!

> *Because the Sovereign Lord helps me, I will not be disgraced.*
> Isaiah 50:7

I said *yes* to His Lordship and His prompting, and He did the work:
- I repented of my distrust in Him. I was afraid that, if the divorce were to happen, it would show that He didn't care or wasn't able to stop it, but I was not destroyed, as I had feared.
- I was actively grateful for the beautiful grace He had been showering on me. I was thankful I had more than survived yet another storm. That's pretty awesome!
- His grace allowed me to make mistakes. I didn't have to pray or worship perfectly or be like someone else. I learned that I could stumble, and He would keep me from falling. He wasn't judging or being critical of all my thoughts and words.
- I worshiped Him morning, noon, and night in all states of emotion.
- I chose joy in my purpose and did not affirm my present condition.
- I esteemed myself in terms of where I was going, not of how I was doing. This created an atmosphere for joy to blossom.

- I believed that He was working all things out for my good, and I hunted for evidence of that every day.
- I was developing new, godly thinking patterns.
- I was choosing obedience and showing trust by simply turning to Him again and again, asking for help not in anger, not with complaining, and not with bargaining—just running to His arms.
- I treasured having been given a heart of compassion, grace, and empathy for my wife. I didn't understand it all, but I knew that there was a war in the spirit world trying to destroy a family, along with each of us individually. Three birds with one stone! I knew Satan was on the scene and that my vows of "for better or for worse" meant that I needed to fight while my spouse couldn't. I repeat, I was "given" a gift of grace at this time. This did not come from my natural heart.

This last point has kept me in the Word and on my knees, searching for more of God, more grace, more understanding, and less confusion. It was hard to sit still (little did I understand!), but agape love is an act of the will. In my obedience, resentment was not finding a foothold, and my felt need for vindication was not taking root. Forgiveness and gratefulness flooded my soul in their place. This gift had become bigger to me than the realization of what my prodigal had done, which grew in me a posture of deepening love, a growing perception of her as precious and honored in my sight.

> Love under accuses, over repents, and over forgives.
> It takes faith to forgive. This is from God.

I was now standing with one foot in my condition and one foot in my position (Isaiah 6). I was not denying where I was but was trying to wrap my heart around what could be. Looking back, I thank God for His grace to equip me with so many resources to fight with at the very start of this wonderful journey.

This is still not a duty assignment or battle plan I fully understand. As I said before, if I had been aware beforehand of the twists and turns of "standing," I might not have started the process. It has been painful. Despite my having done many right things and knowing that God was pleased with my faith, I hurt and wept a great deal. In the beginning I would often ask God to remove this assignment if it were not from Him—"Take it—I can't handle the pain." The answer always came back, "And after you have done everything, stand." I couldn't shake it.

If this is a place in which you find yourself, you may feel very alone when you self-identify to your friends as a "stander." Well-intentioned people have told me to just let God heal my memories, to move on and allow time to heal all my wounds. That didn't resonate with me.

God has given me a burden for my promised one and for our marriage. A burden is a difficult charge, requiring effort to heft. I am sharing the hurt and pain her spirit is experiencing from turning away from God. This is a hurt that time alone will not heal. It is hungry for attention every day. Some days it recedes a bit, but it is always present, like Hannah's burning heart in chapter one of 1 Samuel.

What if you were certain that someone close to you was reacting to situations and basing their reality on their past experiences? We all do that to a certain extent, right? Even unknowingly, if you had a heart that gave and received love from guarded and protective conditioning, wouldn't you need generous margins in your relationships? Of course. You would need love and compassion, not judgment. That is the mature and Christ-like response I am seeking to grow in my life—to offer compassion and grace without judgment. In fact, this is what we all need and what God will supply in abundance in our lives if we allow Him.

Above all, love each other deeply, because love covers over a multitude of sins.

1 Peter 4:8

It was with joy that Jesus volunteered for a difficult mission and endured the cross for our sake. Hebrews 12:2 (BSB) encourages us to reach for the high calling of God each day:

Let us fix our eyes on Jesus, the author and perfecter of our faith, who for the joy set before him endured the cross, scorning its shame, and sat down at the right hand of the throne of God.

Chapter 4

Wait, This *Is* about Her, Isn't It?

Nope. I wanted it to be. I believed that my words, actions, and motives had all been rooted in love (well, mostly)—and she had still left me. I had been the good guy this time. I was spiritually aligned, as I was the one pursuing God. She was the one running! (Translation: I didn't want any eyes on me.) It's, oh, so easy to point our finger at the wrongs in others. I do it too often. There must be a villain somewhere, and I know it's not me.

It is good that God can see into all hearts and minds and see through all our blind spots and misperceptions. Unfortunately, without Him none of us is inherently very good at considering "all things" when someone else is up in our business.

Remarkably, I was left without options to which I could point my finger. Hurting to such an extent, I sought God for validation with the intent to clear my name. In doing so, I did receive affirmation of my name and who I was, and this freed me of shame and judgment.

In addition, His staff consoled me, while His rod comforted me in loving discipline to show that He cares about all the facets that comprise me. I experienced His ability to shine light into previously darkened places by His Spirit of truth, guiding me into understanding.

> *The unfolding of your words gives light; it gives understanding to the simple.*
> Psalm 119:130

God wants a reconciliation *in* Him, not just *between* me and my wife. He wants restoration and healing to wholeness, not a festering wound with a band-aid on it. Revival to new life is stronger and more God-glorifying than sustaining old life. That is why, in our own impatience and weakness, my wife and I experienced several false starts in trying to make a re-marriage happen. All things were not yet new.

I wanted the words of St. Augustine to be true: "Give me chastity and temperance—but not yet!" This was not the time to turn the light on me to fix my issues. But truth began to stare me in the face. I had fewer places to hide. I wasn't looking to hide, mind you, but I had my own versions of truth that were being challenged. Therefore, when God was asking me to follow Him, there was no one else in the room He was asking to step forward. God had me in a place to listen, and my heart was in a place to receive. I allowed Him to make this journey be about me, to begin challenging and changing me.

Two questions took form in my spirit:
1. Was there anything in my life that would hinder God's healing of my marriage?
2. What changes did I need to make in my life to be the kind of husband my returning spouse would need me to be for her?

There is necessary introspection all of us need to do to check the condition of our heart. The apostle Peter experienced the enemy as a prowling, roaring lion seeking to devour and recognized that even he was not safe in his own strength.

Soon after Peter had boldly stated that Jesus was "the Christ of God," Jesus said to him in Luke 22:31–32, "'*Simon, Simon, Satan has asked to sift you as wheat. But I have prayed for you, Simon, that your faith may not fail. And when you have turned back, strengthen your brothers.*'" Following this, Simon Peter experienced the worst moments of his life when he denied, on three occasions, that he even knew Jesus. The enemy will exploit our weaknesses!

Jesus confronted Peter's heart while speaking encouragement into his life. If Jesus were standing in front of me, I have no doubt that He would confront me with the same truth and encouragement—that God will not let me live below that which He has called me to be. He has plans for me that I have not yet seen, heard, or imagined.

Maybe my journey wasn't about changing my prodigal so much as it was about changing my heart to stay faithful and not quit.

The best hope for change in another person is to let God change me. Using it to bring me to a place that I would never have reached on my own.

As the Luke 15 Bible parable plays out in my life, it speaks numerous truths and takes on many dimensions. It grows my belief in an active and dependable Father, as He empowers me to emulate the prodigal's father. Not by shaming me for my shortcomings but by nourishing my desire to change. He affirms my value to Him and His kingdom: to be a part of His redemptive plan by facing and trusting Him.

I encourage you to read the short Old Testament book of Ruth from your Bible. The sovereignty of our great God is clearly seen in this account, which highlights integrity, righteousness, and faithfulness. God guided Ruth every step of the way to become His child and fulfill His plan for her to ultimately become an ancestor of Jesus Christ.

We read that Ruth was in a tough situation, but she did not make it about herself. Her inspiring words: "I will go where you go and die where you die." God turned a hopeless situation and made it into something glorious for her, Naomi, Boaz, ... and ultimately the world.

Ruth could have thought about her needs above all else but instead demonstrated loyalty. That sounds a bit wide-eyed and unsophisticated these days. But that's what Christ's love does. That kind of love in us endures many hardships, even with joy, to complete another's life and faith!

May the God of endurance and encouragement grant you to live in such harmony with one another, in accord with Christ Jesus,
 that together you may with one voice glorify the God and Father of our Lord Jesus Christ.

Romans 15:5–6 (ESV)

Chapter 5

Burden—the Weight of Waiting in Hope

Carry each other's burdens, and in this way you will fulfill the law of Christ.

Galatians 6:2

Burden.

Let's see what this churchy word is about. It's typically used as a noun, yet for some time it has come to weigh heavily on me in verb form. It's from that perspective that I share.

bur·den /ˈbərd(ə)n/ verb: that which is borne with difficulty; obligation on us.

In marriage, there are times when love calls you to share or even carry your mate's burdens. No surprise there. When the weight of "stuff" is depleting your mate's hope, you help bear their burden. When they question their ability to move into the future without looking back with regret, you bear their burden. When they struggle with their identity, you bear their burden. When their physical health challenges them, you bear their burden. When they worry about money, kids, and the future, you help carry their burden.

We feel the burdens of those we love. Their disappointments, fears, tears, and worries inadvertently affect us. Their struggles, concerns, and challenges will, in some part, transfer to our own shoulders. While we allow this in love, it is often a weighty sacrifice, as we have our own "stuff" to deal with. However, we do it, as we remember that we are carrying someone else's heavy load that they might not be able to carry at that time. I've learned, however, that God has a purpose in it because of the great love He has for us and our loved ones. While entering the suffering of others, we can experience this God-designed privilege of offering compassion, even while laying aside our own burdens.

> *But rejoice inasmuch as you participate in the sufferings of Christ, so that you may be overjoyed when his glory is revealed.*
> 1 Peter 4:13

When a burden grows to the point that it feels too heavy to carry, it becomes necessary to admit this truth and to call out to God for help. We look for answers, but if none comes it is easy to allow discouragement to engulf us. Crying out for relief is all we can do. These struggles can become very frustrating and confusing when, in our calling out to God, we dare to admit the feeling that He seems absent. Against all our knowledge and hope, it appears as though He is nowhere to be found. In these times it's all we can do to not get caught up in fruitless mental gymnastics that only seem to add to the problem.

This confusing, silent weight of waiting has been a very real experience for me—one that has forced me many times to throw another log on the fire and ruminate. I run to God's Word and take solace in the company of David, the psalmist, and, of course, I am reminded of the supreme struggle of the Son of God on the cross, crying out to His Father, and am prompted to remember that this struggle is common to all. When I feel myself to be sinking below the waves, the Scriptures come alive on every page, and I experience God's outstretched arms bountifully providing comfort and hope for a more glorious time!

> *In all this you greatly rejoice, though now for a little while you may have had to suffer grief in all kinds of trials.*
> *These have come so that the proven genuineness of your faith—of greater worth than gold, which perishes even though refined by fire—may result in praise, glory and honor when Jesus Christ is revealed.*
> 1 Peter 1:6–7

Carrying a burden means staying until the work is done, carrying on with endurance. Otherwise, the other person is no better off than if you had not helped them in the first place. To truly bear a burden is to be willing to walk with and stand by another person to the very end. The focus is to lighten the weight that someone else is struggling to carry. Aaron and Hur did this for Moses in Exodus 17 to help secure a victory over their enemy.

God hasn't *gently laid* this burden of my promised one on me. He thrust it on me! It hasn't appeared to be an optional assignment. I've had to grapple with the implications and the how-to of it, especially with my bride being AWOL.

What is God's intention in giving me this arduous burden, challenging my faith, and encouraging my prayers in this? I'm learning that God uses His children in partnership. He wants to use us as "vessels" for His purposes. He has helped me to understand that a vessel is used to both fill and to pour from, thereby strengthening both the vertical relationship and the horizontal relationship. That's a beautiful thing.

> "God does nothing except in response to believing prayer."
> —*John Wesley*

My prodigal made a free will choice to go into the far country. We all do this to varying degrees. I have dissected, wrestled with, and reassembled this free will thing a lot.

We know that God is a gentleman and that He respects our free will. So, why is God burdening me with a hope for restoration when He is going to allow my prodigal to freely walk in the other direction? Since it is not often that someone will voluntarily change their heart and turn from their path, this would seem to be a fruitless and painful approach.

The scriptural truth is that God can and does change hearts. I also know this from personal experience—He changed *my* direction—and I believe He can interrupt my prodigal's path. As the years pass and I see no evidence indicating a change in her, however, the knowledge that He will do this does test my faith.

The following reasoning was new to me and gave me hope by helping me understand God's relentless pursuit for our attention. There is a law of gravity. How then do airplanes fly? There is also a law of aerodynamics. Through the latter law, the airplane doesn't negate or break the former law; it just supersedes it for a time.

Comparably, God follows His own law of free will. He does not do away with it while He works to change our hearts, but He can guide or bend our will through time and circumstances. We begin to see the error of our decisions and realize that He has a better way. He makes us willing without going against our free will by leading our heart and opening the door for us to walk through.

Some subscribe to another line of reasoning I am still wrestling with: when God gave us dominion over the earth, He placed himself in a moral position whereby He must respect our free wills before He acts in our sphere of responsibility. The psalmist tells us in Psalm 115:16 (NASB1995), *"The heavens are the heavens of the Lord, But the earth He has given to the sons of men."* This thinking concludes that our prayers are giving God an avenue to override our disobedient hearts. He uses our partnership with Him to influence the hearts of others.

Don't think for a minute that I have this 100% figured out! Entering the suffering of others so they can be changed is true intercession. My burden-bearing morphs from weighty prayers into worship full of emotionally charged devotion expressed in song. Many facets of my soul and spirit come together to stand in hope.

This all-encompassing effort has presented a few issues for me to work through. First, I sometimes wrestle with the question of whether my burden has become an idol. Am I focusing an unhealthy, continuous attention on it? Am I starting to let it define who I am? Have I released and trusted my prodigal entirely to God, or am I still trying to hold on to some control? Does it show that I am not receiving God's rest?

The Lord sent me to Joshua 1. My reading stopped at verse 13: *"The Lord your God will give you rest by giving you this land."*

I must have been doing something wrong. I was not receiving rest from my burden. Fortunately, I picked up and continued reading. The chapter continues to describe a full-scale battle, with fully armed soldiers God was requiring before his returning children received entrance into the promised land. The land would not be handed over without their involvement. Victory would involve fighting for it. That didn't sound to me like rest!

When we read God's Word with a searching heart, our faith (believing) comes from our hearing. This faith then moves us to become more obedient, which encourages us to listen even more. This cycle grows our intimacy with God. Likewise, as we trust Him with our burdens and worries, we experience His faithfulness from the rest and refreshment He lavishes on us.

In Galatians 6:2 I read that the apostle Paul exhorts us to *"Carry each other's burdens."* This contrasts with the individualized load of verse 5, *"for each one should carry their own load."* Verse 2 burdens are those extra heavy loads or situations that are difficult to endure by oneself. Charles Spurgeon clarifies verse 5:

> "Every man shall bear his own burden." That is, if you and I are saved, we must each one have a work of his own, and we must set to work, and do it personally. The Lord has put each one of us into a position where there is something we can do which nobody else can do, and we are bound to do it, and not to begin thinking of how little others do, or how much others do, but to say to our Lord, "What wilt thou have me to do?" Let each Christian Levite bow his shoulder and carry some burden for the Lord's house.

I interpret this to mean to bear your share, so faith can come nearer to outsiders.

This quote resonated, but I needed to understand more on this subject. My initial belief in Christianity assumed that my actions and deeds were what was required for me to be loved by God. Through growth I have realized that, had I continued in that belief, I would be carrying this heavy burden up the mountain by myself.

I read about all of Paul's trials and burdens in 2 Corinthians 11 and then read this verse that Jesus spoke:

> *"A new command I give you: Love one another. As I have loved you, so you must love one another."*
> John 13:34

Jesus joyfully carried a gigantic burden for all of us because He loved us. Paul was tested beyond comprehension. I had to admit that I have much to learn about burden bearing, yet I know I can commit my burdens to God, and I ask Him to strengthen me in the process.

The second question I had about my burden had to do with the fact that I had exhibited some rescuer traits in the past: Can carrying someone else's burden show that I am acting out of helper or rescuer tendencies?

Helping is assisting someone to do something for themselves. A rescuer, on the other hand, is a liberator who acts on an internal need to help. A rescuer takes on the responsibilities, burdens, and problems of other people, thereby saving another from the consequences of their own actions. The rescuer connects their own self-worth to being needed and taking care of others.

It didn't take long for me to dismiss this idea. My worth is found in Jesus and no one else. He set the price by what He paid for me—death on the cross. My true hope is in Him alone. I no longer see myself in the role of a rescuer. Jesus's role, through the Holy Spirit, is that of the only rescuer. I can point and pray, but what is truly needed is my bowed and yielded heart. My desire is to reflect God's agape love and to be an encourager to that end.

He reached down from on high and took hold of me; he drew me out of deep waters.

He rescued me from my powerful enemy, from my foes, who were too strong for me.

They confronted me in the day of my disaster, but the Lord was my support.

He brought me out into a spacious place; he rescued me because he delighted in me.

Psalm 18:16–19

Many waters cannot quench love; rivers cannot sweep it away. If one were to give all the wealth of one's house for love, it would be utterly scorned.

Song of Songs 8:7

Chapter 6

"What If" Kind of Faith

Faith was not given to us to avoid pain, but to go victoriously through the pain with a renewed appreciation for what we have placed our hope in.

My faith has gone through a marked evolution during my journey. Where I started and where I now am are two different places. God has walked me through this process over time to refine me. I'm sure that He has bigger plans than I can conceive.

My initial struggles and questions reflected my unsure footing. I was groping for some bedrock for my faith to stand on: What if my prodigal was heavy on my heart for a reason? What if God did intervene and work all things together for my—for *our*—good? What if God were using this trial for something I could not yet see? What if something impossible for me *is* possible with God?

This is a "what if" kind of faith. I felt the Lord leading me in this, and, though I didn't see where He wanted me to step next, I did believe He would be there for me. I prayed, "God, I'm willing to believe you can answer my prayer!"

Contemplating the cross of Jesus moved me from thinking of His self-sacrifice--the "foolishness of the cross" (1 Corinthians 1:18)—to seeing it in the context of His resurrection. Suddenly, the "what if" of the gospel was full of possibilities of the power that is available to each of us every day. Purpose was planted but had not yet germinated.

The roller-coaster nature of my marriage for several years prior to our split had seemed to have a despairingly long duration. I never imagined that years later I would still be mired in confusion and hurt. I loved this woman and was committed to finding a path forward for us. I was nowhere near ready to quit and did not want to let her go. But she had made it clear that I didn't have a choice in the matter, as she had retreated into her "far country." I had drawn the proverbially "Chute" card in this real-life game of Chutes and Ladders, and it slid me down a chute back to the bottom of the game board, back to the start. I felt as though I had fallen off the game table of life. Our vacillating relationship after our split only added to my feelings of instability, injustice, and helplessness. It hurt. Deeply. Backed up in a corner, I still believed God had the power to bring about a relationship restoration. So, with nothing else to do or to hold onto, I stepped into a "what if" He would do this for me kind of faith. I was willing to believe *for me*!

God blew on those embers of my fledgling faith because I stayed engaged and trusting in Him. I began with an attitude of "How long will this take?" and it flamed to the point of showing the possibilities of what could be. My faith grew. My hope grew. I reasoned that, if God truly were for me, He had to be there waiting for my next step. This important progress was possible only because I was able to believe and depend on the radical goodness of God. His deep love had released permission in me to dream the unthinkable!

It took some time for me to understand and agree with God's thoughts and the belief He had in me. It seemed that I had a long way to travel before I would resemble the prodigal's father. I had miles to cover and lessons to learn. I prayed for further understanding and guidance. Introspective housecleaning helped to open myself to the Holy Spirit's leading. It was going to take some time "to lean not on my own understanding" and to "submit to Him in all my ways."

Two Scriptures that grabbed me early on and breathed hope and direction into me:

Galatians 6:9—"*Let us not become weary in doing good, for at the proper time will reap a harvest if we do not give up.*" My initial mindset was more along the line of "If I am good enough, she will see the error of her ways, realize I am a good guy, and then come back." Yet, the principle this verse teaches is the exact description of Christ's modeled behavior of always doing the right thing for the benefit of the person standing in front of Him. This was not entirely lost on me, but it has taken some feeding of my faith for me to embrace it.

Galatians 5:6—"*The only thing that counts is faith expressing itself through love.*" Because I had no other options, this verse resonated with me. I desired a pure faith from a heart of pure love. Little did I realize the miles this would add to my journey.

Often, my head seemed awash with jumbled thoughts and feelings. I could be prayed up and very encouraged, and 12 minutes later I'd find myself in the heat of oppression again. The enemy often reminded me that I had been rejected and that my hopes and dreams were baseless, and loneliness was my lot in life. As confusion was sown, my questioning of all things began. This was oppressive some days. During such times my prayers were just groanings.

Yet, at God's request and in His strength, I remained standing. I think I was standing because it was all I knew to do--this posture had become who I was. I stood because doing so was not complex. I stood like a horse in a rainstorm that doesn't have any recourse to come in out of the rain. In my desperate condition, I had nothing to sustain me other than the nourishment of His Word.

As an Ironman triathlete and marathon competitor, I have endured intense training periods during which food to sustain me was all that mattered. I trained so I could then eat so I would live another day. When my coach told me to go ride a bike for seventy miles or run ten miles, or both, one after the other, that's what I did—no questions. I left the methods of my training to my coach. My objective was to get to the food that would nourish me. Food was my focus. Not just any food; my body demanded good, nutritious food--not junk food—for sustained energy. It was aware of and alert to the counterfeit and the inferior.

During my burdensome times of standing, God nourishes me. He prepares a rich table for me in the presence of my adversaries! He sits and sups with me! He restores my soul! He is the real deal, the real sustenance—not counterfeit! I *will* stand in the rain for that!

My "what if" faith had me searching in all places, both in and out of Scripture, to find out if my marriage restoration was a promise of God. Did He promise that my marriage would be restored and healed to wholeness? Do you hear the crickets? Let me save you the time. *That promise is not in Scripture.* Of course, He desires that marriages be restored and that couples enjoy life-giving relationships. But there is another person in the equation, and God is a gentleman. He will not force anyone to love Him and follow His ways if they don't desire to. Pure love requires love to be returned freely.

My "what if" faith had me asking God to remove this burden if I were not acting out of pure love and motivation. If I were not sincere about my love for my promised one, I didn't want to continue in my quest. He did not oblige my request.

Pure faith is not something matured in a short period of time. Though it took effort, I stayed faithful every day, not out of compulsion but out of a hunger for hope. My faith grew. My flesh pushed back at times, tempting me to respond as the prodigal or as his older brother. My past, deep-rooted shame and judgmental view of Christianity would have caused me to fail in the role of the prodigal's father. No way could I have handled faking that kind of abstract, illogical, unfair, and un-American kind of attitude. Love my son after he had selfishly run away? With no consequences or judgment? Surely you jest.

I marvel at God the Father and His desire for wholeness in me as He matures me in our growing relationship. He guides and teaches me the wisdom of the prodigal's father by turning my heart away from any unforgiveness, judgment, bitterness, and anger. My life now has more room to lead with grace.

Why did the prodigal's father stand and persevere for his son's return? Maybe he was considering the "what if" possibilities for a rebellious son who is restored. Maybe, in a trial from his own past, he was refined through grace and was simply reflecting the relentless and steadfast love that his heavenly Father had shown him. This heart and mindset would now invite God's grace and power in to repair the destructive dynamics of his whole family.

Whatever the reason, the biblical prodigal came home.

Chapter 7

"Even If" Kind of Faith

This thought came to me—What if I never again am afforded the opportunity to show my faith to God like I have during this journey? Wow, kind of makes me think I ought to do this right.

My "what if" faith had a sidekick named "as long as" faith. I befriended him as well. We all know the bargaining we do with God: "As long as you (God) answer me in a reasonable amount of time . . . as long as you work it out like I think it needs to work out . . . as long as I don't go through any pain . . . I will have faith in you."

Soon I realized that this approach was creating an idol in me. I had fashioned a view of God in terms of the way I thought He should look and act (there's a good Bible study right there). I wanted Him to do this my way, but I again encountered the sovereign God of creation, who came to overthrow the kingdom of darkness—something I had little experience in. I am sure He valued my input, but His purposes were beyond my reasoning, and thus above my pain.

As I continued to pursue God, my faith was maturing, and my conviction of the depths of God's trustworthiness and His promise of working all things for my good was growing in me as well. I stepped from a "what if" faith into an "even if" kind of faith. "Even if" faith strengthens me to take the punches and still come back to the fight because I see that God is trustworthy. Building trust in God always moves us in one direction—"Not my will, but yours." Even if it is painful, even if we are confused, even if we are disappointed, He is trustworthy. Growing trust in Him grows our desire to be more obedient, and obedience is less painful when we are in love with Jesus.

These were new thinking patterns that I needed to flesh out. I was still experiencing hurt, disappointment, and confusion, so "Why is all this happening?" seemed to still be a very valid question. Scripture teaches that Jesus is the author and perfector of my faith. So, I took my search to God—not to my old thinking patterns and not to Google.

> *Draw near to God, and he will draw near to you. Cleanse your hands, you sinners, and purify your hearts, you double-minded.*
>
> James 4:8 (ESV)

Waiting for my promised one is *hard*—likely the hardest thing I'll ever do, as it stretches me in ways I could never have imagined. As I pray for this seemingly unbearable journey to end, I cry. Tears have become my food.

What journey of faith did the prodigal's father go through? How often did he gaze longingly down the road? Did his chest tighten and his breathing slow as tears welled in his eyes yet again? Why had his son left home? Did the unwelcome thought of a forever lost son ever intrude itself in a weak moment and unleash a sobbing release? Such details are not part of this Bible parable. I doubt the father could have responded to his son's return with so much grace, joy, and forgiveness had he not often watered the seeds of his hope and faith along the way with his tears.

Did the prodigal's father have to remind himself of God's trustworthiness "even if" he had to push back against any shame or feelings of failure for having raised such a son? Did the father have to endure scorn from townspeople for making a radical decision like giving his son his inheritance while he was still alive? How did people greet him in the streets while the son was away? Did they avert their eyes, not wanting to be close to such a sordid family affair? Did the father's peers try to give him advice on how they would have handled the situation? Did they murmur amongst themselves when the son returned, watching the father run out to meet him and throw a party for an unrighteous child who had been flaunting his sin?

God's promises are still valid "even if" I face struggles. Here are the top five struggles I have had to battle against:

1. Did God really say, "Stand for my marriage"?

2. The quietness of God
3. The waiting
4. Wanting to help God do His job
5. Wearing my burden

Did God really say, "Stand for my marriage"?

> Doubt always coexists with faith.

"God, did you really say *that*?" The oldest trick to sow confusion into our lives goes all the way back to the serpent in the garden. The enemy is not always original, but he is effective in getting us to question our hearing of God's voice. Yes, God did say that—and He meant it! Why, I asked, did I have to have Him keep repeating it? Sometimes His reminder would calm me for several days; at other times it was for mere minutes, after which I was again crying out for Him to verify whatever it was I needed. We are feeble, sheep-like, fleshly humans. The deceiver knows this and has this question queued up on our top ten playlist. You will hear that question as well if you are standing for anything that God is calling you to do.

I reread God's Word often until I finally believed the truth about His character and recognized the deceit the enemy was using to keep me off balance. I have learned how to reply, "Get behind me, Satan. God really did say that!" and I have learned how to rebuke Satan and his lies in Jesus's name. Often, I just laugh while shutting him down. These methods have been effective . . . and kind of fun! Over time it does get easier to recognize God's voice. God is patient, and how glad I am for that.

While God has never promised me a restored marriage (maybe others have been given this promise), He did verify that this had been a covenant marriage and that He wanted it to stay intact to honor Him. He hates divorce. I no longer listen to the lies of, "Well, you both are probably happier this way," "She wasn't meant to be in your life," or "It's just not worth the pain."

The quietness of God

Isaiah 45:15 in the ESV tells us, *"Truly you are a God who hides himself."*

Seriously, a perplexing Scripture. Why is God so reticent at times when I need Him so much? In my case, He hasn't been silent, but let's just say He wouldn't always be a great dinner date. I'm learning the answer; I just don't like the process:

> To show me how utterly dependent I am on God's grace and presence.

Silence, The Lord's love language.

The best work God does in me is when He seems the farthest away.

Silence is a testing of my faith to prove myself to me.

What? Sometimes I just shake my head at such wisdom, but I keep digging and asking, still groping for answers and truth. I've called out and sought the Holy Spirit so many times, seeking the Lord's direction from 1,000 different angles with 10,000 different questions. Yet, no matter how often I've wanted to hear Him, He has remained mostly silent.

In just a few days the belief of Mary and Martha was sorely tested, and their confusion became overwhelming (John 11). Their brother, Lazarus, had taken ill and was close to death. In faith they sent word to Jesus, their close friend and Teacher, to come and heal "the one you love." In Jesus's delay, Lazarus died, after which Jesus said this to His disciples who were with Him: *"Lazarus has died, and for your sake I am glad that I was not there"* (verses 14–15 ESV), meaning present to heal Lazarus. The story further unfolds with the reason for the purposeful delay: *"so that you may believe,"* and to show the glory of God and His power even over death.

In hindsight, this kind of revelatory truth does provide us with much to wrestle with and coaxes our faith upward, but in the *middle* of our calamity this is not what we are looking for—"I am glad I was not there." Really? When all is pressing in from every side with no answers appearing, I need God with me; I need His very real presence and care!

Think about the long stretch of silence Abraham endured. Twenty-five years of the enemy probing, "Did God really say that?" Abraham possibly experienced thoughts similar to mine: "God, can you please say that again and speak a little louder?"

Simply, God seems to have me on a long leash, which can be disconcerting when I am looking for Him. Wilderness experiences wear me down, causing fatigue and confusion, but I am learning that faith fatigue is part of being a believer. I know God is pleased that I am searching for His presence and recognizing my dependance on Him, but I certainly would like to hear more from Him.

I try to make the best possible decisions with my limited knowledge and sight, but I still ask, "Why is the Lord so quiet?" While fighting for understanding and against confusion in my silence, amazingly, I do experience a very real assurance that He is right next to me, listening and engaged. I fully recognize that the refreshing and the restoring I experience, even in the middle of my wilderness, are a gift from Him encouraging my continued trust.

Oswald Chambers relates silence from God to intimacy with Him: "A wonderful thing about God's silence is that His stillness is contagious—it gets into you, causing you to become perfectly confident so that you can honestly say, 'I know that God has heard me.' His silence is the very proof that He has.... If Jesus Christ is bringing you into the understanding that prayer is for the glorifying of His Father, then He will give you the first sign of His intimacy—silence."

In His silence, maybe God is saying to me, "I'm putting you in a place where you can't see Me, but if you just do what I have asked of you and trust Me that I will do what I have promised to do, I will bring you closer to Me."

Also from Oswald Chambers:

Has God trusted me with His silence—a silence that has great meaning? God's silences are actually His answers. Just think of those days of absolute silence in the home at Bethany! Is there anything comparable to those days in my life? Can God trust me like that, or am I still asking Him for a visible answer?... His silence is the sign that He is bringing me into an even more wonderful understanding of Himself. Am I mourning before God because I have not had an audible response? When I cannot hear God, I will find that He has trusted me in the most intimate way possible—with absolute silence, not a silence of despair, but one of pleasure, because He saw that I could withstand an even bigger revelation. If God has given me silence, then praise Him—He is bringing me into the mainstream of His purposes. The actual evidence of the answer in time is simply a matter of God's sovereignty. Time is nothing to God. For a while you may have said, "I asked God to give me bread, but He gave me a stone instead" (see Matthew 7:9). He did not give you a stone, and today you find that He gave you the "bread of life" (John 6:35).

I remind myself of two pieces of advice that Joyce Meyer gives in one of her books:
- When you don't hear His voice, keep doing what He told you the last time you did hear Him.
- If you are not hearing God, maybe He trusts you with the path you are on.

I did hear the message. God's silence was my opportunity to remain faithful, even when I was unsure of His intentions in my life. Nevertheless, I still had to work through my human desire to hear more from Him, which at times felt like I was striving, pressing too hard. It was clear that I needed to feed my trust and not this root of unbelief.

I have incorporated many long wilderness hikes with a thankful heart and a praise song on my lips, or I have simply sat with a cup of hot tea, listening to background worship music while contemplating the goodness of God. While I haven't heard Him say, "Good job, Ed. Soldier on—you're getting close, and I'll have this wrapped up by the holidays," His Spirit does affirm the many truths I am feeding myself—that He is bending down listening to me; that He is close to the brokenhearted; and clearly, that He overcame sin and death through His Beloved Son so that I might live in victory.

> *"Have I not commanded you? Be strong and courageous. Do not be afraid; do not be discouraged, for the Lord your God will be with you wherever you go."*
>
> Joshua 1:9

Just because we can't hear God singing doesn't mean he is not rejoicing over us with songs of joy. A blind or deaf child may not see their father's face or hear his words, but they can learn to sense his love and affection, nonetheless. Silence is the Lord's love language, growing us from the beauty of discipline to the glory of deliverance. Be disciplined today to be trusted with deliverance tomorrow.

"Even If" Kind of Faith

The waiting

The attack against our hope while in God's waiting room is very much the same strategy that the enemy uses when old, familiar voices try to fill the void of God's silence. Satan likes to remind us that there was some security and stability while we were in our previous strongholds of doubt and distrust. I am very hopeful and full of expectation for God's inevitable victory in my trial; however, waiting remains difficult.

Do you remember when you were a child and your family went on a long car trip to some very exciting place like Disney World? "How much farther?" you asked for the zillionth time. "Be patient—we're getting closer," you were told. What you heard, or what you believed you heard, was, "It's just around the next corner." And then another corner went by. You had complete trust that you were going to Disney World, but you wavered a bit on the timeline.

In my expectation I have "images" of myself with my prodigal. I imagine the wonderful places I want to show her as I travel around this great land, and I also see us having a meal or a long walk together. Is this too real for you? Are you thinking I need to get a grip and get a life? I think that same thought frequently between my bouts of tears, and I protest, "God, there has to be a better way!"

I groan in prayer and ask Him to use my pain for some redemptive purpose—and I thank Him for my tears. Then I look down the road for the next corner.

The rationale for waiting for an answer to my prayers is something I can intellectually understand. I can grasp the principle of spiritual fruit maturing as I wait. I've waited a long time already, and I can wait some more, but the incessant nature of waiting is like looking down the road trying hard to accept that there will yet be another corner ahead.

Sometimes when I am earnestly praying, I ask God for some indications that help is on the way. I'm looking for some breadcrumbs to sustain me for another day. God does provide in several areas that show me that I am in His will, which greatly encourages me and makes the waiting easier (also see the next chapter):

- I am grateful for everything, and I express this to Him continually. I am aware of His care and provision in all things and am thankful I am receiving blessings of all kinds. Life seems

- Scriptures, devotionals, and sermons affirm me rather than just encouraging me. What I mean is that I often am not having to "work" to motivate myself to experience the noble point of some message—I am seeing it made plain in my daily walk.
- I am at peace. I sleep well. I can look myself in the mirror. I feel affirmed, and I feel content. The result is a great joy that God renews every day. This has not left me.

to come together more easily, and I am not having to force things. Problems do not feel as stressful as I develop a different perspective on life.

These breadcrumbs top off my hope tank and make waiting less difficult as I grow more confident that God is pleased with my path, not because I am doing everything right but because I am pursuing His heart.

Though I am buffeted in this storm I am in, I am not afraid of my boat capsizing. The Holy Spirit confirms again and again that my standing and praying for my promised one and our marriage are within His will. This encourages me to persevere and pray for the tough times she may be experiencing. My temporary troubles are worth waiting through because God is in my waiting.

My waiting expresses a faith that says, "Even if I am uncomfortable because I am not in control, I put my hope in God." This "active patience" is the time when God will shape and define us the most.

The Israelites had to wait for the promised land, but everything about Egypt had to first die in their lives. They had to be delivered from the spirit of bondage and their slave mentality, which, though it included feelings of worthlessness, had also provided the only security they'd ever known as slaves. Their self-centered view of what a deliverer, a king, or even God could do for them limited their potential and needed to be refined out of them, as fire refines or purifies gold (Isaiah 48:10).

We all share in some of these self-limiters, and this refining process often takes a while for us. Trust these truths: God is *always* at work, and He is *always* on time. His timing is perfect.

> *For the revelation awaits an appointed time; it speaks of the end and will not prove false. Though it linger, wait for it; it will certainly come and will not delay.*
>
> Habakkuk 2:3

I also believe that my wait is necessary while God is orchestrating people and events—a divine delay for a divine alignment for ultimate goodness. I wait for an outcome that has, number one, God's blessing on it.

> *I will stand at my watch and station myself on the ramparts; I will look to see what he will say to me, and what answer I am to give to this complaint.*
>
> Habakkuk 2:1

I take solace hiking in the mountains, seeking solitude, and having a talk with The Holy Spirit. Maybe these mountains are my ramparts. Or maybe this helps me to look further down the road past the next curve.

Wanting to help God do His job

The near total blackout of communication from my prodigal is heart wrenching. Of course, I want to reach out and comfort and encourage her. I also know that we each have ownership of our own lives and can experience intimidation when it feels as though others are attempting to wrest control. That is not my purpose, but I am also aware of the power of my tongue when used unwisely.

How will she know where my heart is and that it is a safe place to return to? I have written many, many encouraging and uplifting emails that I thought she needed to hear. I want her to know that I feel her pain and am praying for her. Very rarely do I hit the Send key because I'm not confident that what I say through my own effort will change her heart; so, once again, I place her in God's hands. He is looking beyond her brokenness for a return to Him—not for rescuer tactics from me.

This battle belongs to God, and He has asked me to stand firm and be still. Read about Jahaziel's encouragement to Judah's army in 2 Chronicles 20:15-22.

I don't have all the answers in this area, but I want to be sensitive to what the Spirit is doing and not contaminate it. Not once have I checked my prodigal's social media. I don't follow her or keep tabs on her. I have had very few contacts with her. Wisdom tells me that it is best that I know little of what is going on in her life; otherwise, I would be drawn in to fixate on it and worry and not trust God.

I operate from my firm belief that this will not end in death:

> *When he heard this, Jesus said, "This sickness will not end in death. No, it is for God's glory so that God's Son may be glorified through it."*
> John 11:4

I can only surmise why she has had no contact with me. I do know that my current pain is not close to the pain and uncertainty she can only be experiencing. I know because I was a prodigal. I know that shame, guilt, or condemnation don't come from a person but from high places, and my experience was that I couldn't fathom that someone would ever forgive me when I was running. I can still have communion with her in the Spirit world. She can dishonor the covenant but not break it. The prodigal son was still a son.

> *"Come out from them and be separate, says the Lord. Touch no unclean thing, and I will receive you."*
> 2 Corinthians 6:17

Whether it is Abram and Lot agreeing to separate or Paul admonishing Christians to be separate from the values and idols of this world, the Scriptures speak in many places of "being separate." God wants to protect us from the influences that dilute our courage to operate in faith. I have learned that the group (family, friends, social media . . .) is not all going to go along with my faith journey and that support will thin even more the further I proceed because they don't see the purpose or understand it. There will be a loneliness "even if" we are doing what God is asking us to do.

I can see that my leaving town is an appointed separation from the environment I was in. I can appreciate that God wants to operate separately on my prodigal and me and to keep me from being influenced by both bad advice and well-meaning "help." It's not about me doing nothing; it's about my doing what God is calling me to do and using the tools He has given me. This enables me to let my "Yes be yes" to Him. Seeking, serving, writing, and traveling are keeping me positively engaged, so I am not focusing on my pain. God is calling into me what He wants me to be, and He is calling out of her what He wants her to see and receive.

Wearing my burden

This has been my biggest "even if I-have-to-face . . ." struggle: It's not about "why" I have a burden but about how I wear it, about how I carry my disposition each day, about how I differentiate my feelings from God's intended positioning of me for growth.

Without a doubt, this burden has a hold on me. I feel it every day. The popular advice is to talk about it, to let it out. Though I am mostly quiet about my journey, out of respect for my prodigal wife, I do sometimes share some details with a few trusted friends whom I feel will encourage me, grieve with me, be honest with me, and provide a safe place for me to process out loud. I still need this release valve, though not as often.

Thankfully, God is very faithful helping me to carry the burden. I wake up renewed and joyful most days. On the occasional mornings when I must fight for my joy, God is ready to meet me and provide great encouragement. My heart is heavy, yet it is simultaneously glad. How does one wear this kind of burden? Do I drink sorrow and joy from the same cup? Yes!

> To grieve deeply and rejoice relentlessly at the same time is a mark of Christian maturity.

My days are productive, providing a good outlet for me, but in the evening when I shut my RV door is when the challenge is most difficult. I profoundly know that I am alone, and it's easy at those times to become melancholic. I'm reminded that there are still corners ahead in my journey to steer through. Serving in the ministries I do involves traveling and experiencing many new places. This can erode my feelings of stability. So, I purpose my time and attention on God. I determine to trust God for as long as it takes. I will stay faithful in my walk and continue to knock on heaven's door quite often. I don't believe He is the least disturbed by my frequent knocking. He may even have put it on my heart to write this book to still me. The one answer I do have: *God is sovereign.*

> *May the God of hope fill you with all joy and peace as you trust in him, so that you may overflow with hope by the power of the Holy Spirit.*
> Romans 15:13

Chapter 8

"No Matter What" Kind of Faith

What God does in you while you wait might be just as important as, if not more important than, what you're waiting for.

As I continued my faith journey with God, I appreciated that He was growing me to trust Him not only as my maker and provider but also as my Savior and Lord. He wants me to trust Him "no matter what" my need is.

The world wants a loaf of bread for assurance that God is answering their prayers. What if He gives only the breadcrumbs I referenced in the last chapter? Can breadcrumbs sustain our faith "no matter what"? We must not permit the sin of continual doubt to demand that we see the whole loaf first. It's not the doubting that offends God but the letting doubt conquer us and hinder our relationship with Him.

> *Therefore, since we also have such a great cloud of witnesses surrounding us, let's rid ourselves of every obstacle and the sin which so easily entangles us, and let's run with endurance the race that is set before us.*
>
> Hebrews 12:1 (NASB)

Recently I watched a video of what I assumed was a Christian man telling a woman that, since her husband had left her, she should release him—let him go because God had better things for her and because her husband was not the one for her.

I know nothing about that man or the context of the conversation, but my immediate response was a furrowed brow and a check in my spirit (it is important that we are careful with what we allow to infiltrate our minds). Yet, it took only a nanosecond for the enemy to poke me and say, "That's what you are dealing with. Doesn't this apply to you, too?" That lie did get a couple of layers deep into my spirit before I rebuked it and sent it on its way. At least I thought I had. The lie didn't remain, but my mood slightly changed. I cast a backward glance at some of my regrets, and suddenly my joy was not so joyous.

Soon, I sat down for my prayer and study time, and the first verse that I encountered was 1 Corinthians 2:12:

> *What we have received is not the spirit of the world, but the Spirit who is from God, so that we may understand what God has freely given us.*

Then I read my daily devotional on 1 Corinthians 2:14:

> *The person without the Spirit does not accept the things that come from the Spirit of God but considers them foolishness, and cannot understand them because they are discerned only through the Spirit.*

The earlier video was not foremost in my mind when I sat down to study, yet God led me through some truths and a strengthening of my faith on several different levels within just a few minutes. The enemy (remember, that one that is always present, ready to steal, kill, and destroy) will use people, things, or events to persuade us to turn away from what God wants us to do.

We must remember this: the person who is unspiritual will employ reason, will use his senses (his ears, eyes, and unspiritual mind) in trying to "discern" circumstances for what he should do. Reason makes us focus on circumstances, but spiritual discernment helps us see through circumstances.

That which God has given us through His Word and the guidance of the Holy Spirt makes it possible for us to spiritually discern. Therefore, we can have deep confidence about a direction from God, even though it makes no sense in the natural or others may not understand it.

When I become weary of my journey and start listening to the world's voice declaring "move on," "quit," or "you deserve more," I remember the huge, encouraging truth that cemented itself within my spirit, urging me to ignore the world! I remember that spiritual things are spiritually discerned, and I find new refreshment from 1 Corinthians 13:7 (NLT):

> *Love never gives up, never loses faith, is always hopeful, and endures through every circumstance.*

Faith is not an assurance that I will always be able to perceive God. It is a choice to rely upon the fact that God always sees me and is completely faithful in His workings in me. To experience more faith, I must collect evidences in my heart and educate and even reeducate myself with God's truths; I must continue going back to what I have seen and heard and preach to myself and change my thought cycles. This is not a once and done thing. I must be vigilant about removing obstacles that inhibit the growth of my faith. Faith entails a fight! For how long? For as long as it takes, no matter what. God will provide the power of progress in this. At this point in my journey, I really don't know an alternative. Faith pleases God, and it is the foundation of my hope.

> *And without faith it is impossible to please Him, for he who comes to God must believe that He is and that He is a rewarder of those who seek Him.*
>
> Hebrews 11:6 (NASB1995)

In the words of Oswald Chambers,

In learning to walk with God, there is always the difficulty of getting into His stride, but once we have done so, the only characteristic that exhibits itself is the very life of God Himself. The individual person is merged into a personal oneness with God, and God's stride and His power alone are exhibited. Whether a leisurely stroll or an arduous hike, keep in stride with your Savior. Trust the Spirit to lead and one day, He will take you away!

> *Walk in obedience to all that the* Lord *your God has commanded you, so that you may live and prosper and prolong your days in the land that you will possess.*
>
> Deuteronomy 5:33

Faith and hope are gifts from God for trusting Him, and they work together to grow love in us. The reason to love is evident in 1 John 4:7–8; in fact, it is the essence of God:

Dear friends, let us love one another, for love comes from God.

Everyone who loves has been born of God and knows God. Whoever does not love does not know God, because God is love.

Love has the power to help us believe again, and it restores our hope. It is the engine that drives our spiritual lives. The goal is agape love—sacrificial love, not love based on feelings.

And now these three remain: faith, hope and love. But the greatest of these is love.
                                1 Corinthians 13:13

A love that can love the unlovable, the mean neighbor, the sibling who curses us, or the prodigal who has abandoned us. We may be alone or hurt, but we can see the suffering in others and be moved. Our "no matter what" kind of faith enjoys wielding that kind of love by helping people discover God's, and their own, identity—who God is and who they are in God. We all need to hear that when God's grace enters us it tells sin that there is a higher authority and that it won't allow sin to define our identity.

Our stand, our waiting, our calling will allow us to grow in intimacy with our children, our spouse, and others. Standing teaches us to love like Christ. When I pray for people, even hard to love people, I am surprised by the softening of my heart toward them.

The three young Jewish men, Hananiah, Mishael, and Azariah (Shadrach, Meshach, and Abednego), facing certain death in a blazing furnace, manifested a "no matter what" kind of faith:

"If we are thrown into the blazing furnace, the God we serve is able to deliver us from it and he will deliver us from Your Majesty's hand.

> *But even if he does not, we want you to know, Your Majesty, that we will not serve your gods or worship the image of gold you have set up."*
>
> Daniel 3:17–18

I remember my pastor's words, "Don't giveth up," and so I resolve to not serve the god that coaxes me to quit my marriage stand or says my promised one is not worthy of my love, or that she is too giant a burden for me to carry any longer.

My God will deliver me from this, but even if He does not, I will continue to serve Him because He sits on the throne and has an intimate love and devotion for me. Without a doubt, I'll retain not one burn mark, as He will protect me and exult me in due time. Of this I am confident!

It takes discipline to acquire and experience this type of trust: a "no matter what" faith in God's Lordship. The discipline of patience is born of a heart that has learned to wait on the Lord and not be in a hurry to acquire what He knows we will be unable to handle--yet. Waiting requires humble submission and is learned in wilderness experiences where pride is exposed. The discipline of patience is wrought from hearts that are made tender and willing to bow to Jesus as King and Lord.

The book of Job shows God allowing Job to suffer a series of trials that are tough to even read about. God's aim for Job and all of us: to refine our faith, enlarge our holiness, save our soul, and give Him glory.

My chest tightens and my breathing becomes shallow when I read of Job's ordeals. The great deal of unmerited suffering this servant endured proves to all human reasoning that he was one seriously faithful and upright guy. Yet, God bragged about him to Satan before the trouble even started. Why? God already knew his heart and his faith capacity.

Does God boast about us? I think He does when we live a "no matter what" kind of faith. He is pleased with us. He has built in us a warrior He can use for His kingdom purposes.

Chapter 9

Suffering and Perseverance: All Kinds for a Little While

"The broken heart. You think you will die, but you just keep living, day after day after terrible day."

—*Charles Dickens*

"It was the best of times; it was the worst of times."

—*Charles Dickens*

Because this was a tough chapter to write, I started off with two sobering quotations.

It's likely that we all consider ourselves strong enough to endure some suffering in life. Age and life experiences do that for us. Death and divorces make that list for me. My endurance race training did as well. On my hundred-mile bicycle training rides I had words of encouragement printed on my water bottle, staring me in my face as I pedaled on: "Embrace the pain!" That was real suffering. I have backpacked far into the mountains many times, schlepping all my gear up the endless hills. I helped raise five kids—I know about sacrifice and perseverance as well!

The word *suffering* is often synonymous with the word *pain*. It has been said that pain has a purpose and that suffering is a choice. Many Bible translations seem to use the two words interchangeably.

Of course, suffering and pain are universal experiences shared by all of humanity and are products of the fall, a consequence of human sin against God (Romans 5:12; 1 Corinthians 15:21). Suffering is part of our entire lives because we are living in a broken world. Some suffering is due to our sinful and wrong choices, but some is due simply to the world being fallen. Real and authentic suffering is a certainty in our Christian walk. It is not optional.

> "Dear Child of God, I am sorry to say that suffering is not optional."
>
> —*Archbishop Desmond Tutu*

The Bible devotes considerable time and space to the importance of suffering and to how the believer in Christ and His Word is empowered to respond to it. God uses our suffering. His purposes in our suffering are certainly different from the way the unbelieving world views it.

This topic would encompass several books and lots of Scripture to study it more thoroughly. I am going to focus on the suffering that I have personally experienced and how God has brought revelation, growth, obedience, and peace to me as I walk through the valley of the shadow of death (that being anything that is trying to shake or steal my faith).

Call it what you want. When we're on the receiving end, we'd rather change the channel and get rid of the hurt. None of us enjoys suffering. It goes against our flesh. We are not programmed to exclaim, "Bring it on!" We learn to deal with it and manage the best we can. Then we get to the verse in James 1:2:

> *Consider it pure joy, my brothers and sisters, whenever you face trials of many kinds.*

Joyful—really? This truth added more miles to my journey.

My joy had been buried and was being danced on by my hurt and suffering. It was easier to just cry rather than fight for an elusive joy. A broken marriage was bad enough to suffer, but it was the continuous prayerful pursuit of God that had all my focus. It wasn't enough that my prayers were for God to not only bring my promised one to a surrender and bring her home to me but also for her secret hopes of overcoming past hurts to be realized in her life. This was not a small request.

I still pray for her, just as a child would continuously call for her lost pet. At times this brings a heavy pall over me. I hurt. I get on my knees weeping for my loved one. I have marched around the rooms of my home a thousand times singing and praying, waiting for the walls of her divide to come crashing down.

When I first experienced all of this, it was a great deal of weight on my shoulders. I began to see in myself signs of depression. I soon realized that this depression was different from what I had experienced in my past. I was in a spiritual depression. I was crushed in spirit.

As Charles Spurgeon explains:

> Love and self-denial for the object loved go hand-in-hand. If I profess to love a certain person, and yet will neither give my silver nor my gold to neither relieve his needs, nor in any way deny myself comfort or ease for his sake, such love is contemptible. It wears the name, but lacks the reality of love. True love must be measured by the degree to which the person loving will be willing to subject himself to crosses and losses, to suffering and self-denials. After all, the value of a thing in the market is what a man will give for it, and you must estimate the value of a man's love by that which he is willing to give up for it. What will he do to prove his affection? What will he suffer for the sake of benefiting his be-loved? Greater love for friends has no man than this that he lay down his life for them.

God led me to the book of Psalms, and I have never left. The psalms are prayers and songs that allow me to say things I was not sure I could say to God. I see David battling the same adversaries of his feelings and emotions that I was. He pursued God with a desperation and unguarded heart that I could relate to:

> *In my distress I cried unto the Lord, and he heard me.*
> Psalm 120:1 (KJV)

At this point in his life David had a broken heart and was downcast. Not only was he afraid for his physical life, but he was also seeking amends for his sins, as well as hope for his eternal life:

> *The Lord is close to the brokenhearted and saves those who are crushed in spirit.*
> Psalm 34:18

In many places we see David battling spiritual depression, yet he responds from the promise of the incorruptible seed of God's covenant love for him and turns his depression into an opportunity to search, instead, for truth and hope:

> *Why, my soul, are you downcast? Why so disturbed within me? Put your hope in God, for I will yet praise him, my Savior and my God.*
>
> Psalm 42:5

Obviously, God was preparing David's heart for a purpose, a bigger picture for a larger calling:

> *This is my comfort in my affliction, that your promise gives me life.*
>
> Psalm 119:50 (ESV)

Charles Spurgeon expresses his wrestling with depression:

This (spiritual) depression comes over me whenever the Lord is preparing a larger blessing for my ministry; the cloud is black before it breaks and overshadows before it yields its deluge of mercy. Depression has now become to me as a prophet in rough clothing, a John the Baptist heralding the nearer coming of my Lord's richer blessing; so have far better men found it.

Pastor, teacher, and author Gregory Brown has this to say:

Often to find relief from depression, we'll need to pursue God in a heightened fashion for a season. For some, their battle will require them to keep a higher devotion to the Lord than their peers for the rest of their lives to maintain peace. If that is God's will for them, it's actually a blessing because they might never seek God in the same way apart from such a battle with depression. Like God said to Paul, His grace is made perfect in weakness. For those few, God chooses to not remove the thorn in the flesh for a greater purpose (2 Corinthians 12:7–9).

This loving people thing can become a serious struggle until we contemplate that Jesus's sacrifice wasn't just for the easily persuaded. He came to destroy strongholds and fight for the hearts and minds of His children taken captive. His heart is for all of us to live freely in God's will. As with Jesus, our true self and true love are revealed when we give ourselves for another.

Some people in the city of (biblical) Corinth seem to have pointed to Paul's suffering as evidence that he must not have been much of an apostle. After all, wouldn't God intervene to spare a close servant of His from all that pain? This is a common assumption in many false religions: that the true servants of a god are protected from any harm. Even today, this lie persists in those who claim that any Christian who suffers does so because they lack faith.

Paul said that the opposite is true. He believed that God had put his body on display for the world to see two things. First, he wanted people to notice how often he was weak and close to death for the sake of Christ and, second, to notice how powerful Christ showed Himself to be as He continued to fortify Paul's weakened body. This was so that Paul would be able to continue sharing the gospel of the One he loved and to serve more and more people.

Suffering isn't uncommon for any person who is walking with Christ—we will encounter "the enemy of our souls." Suffering takes many forms—spiritual, physical, mental, emotional, relational, or others. But to choose to "endure the suffering of trials and consider it pure joy" was something I had yet to understand. Now say it with me: "Just because I don't understand God's wisdom doesn't negate it; it just means that I don't understand it." God is God and I am not—and in this life I will never fully understand.

It was time for me to increase my understanding of suffering. "Why, God, all this pain?"

C. S. Lewis writes:

> Now God, who has made us, knows what we are and that our happiness lies in Him. Yet we will not seek it in Him as long as He leaves us any other resort where it can even plausibly be looked for. While what we call "our own life" remains agreeable we will not surrender it to Him. What then can God do in our interests but make "our own life" less agreeable to us, and take away the plausible sources of false happiness?

What can you say to that, other than, "Amen!"?

I don't know what to do with this pressure. God's hand is upon me, yet the pressure remains. So, I hold my head in my hands

> and cry, and look for Him. My soul thirsts for Him.
> My foes taunt me, saying, "Where is your God?" My deep knows on which I stand, but my feelings are not satisfied with a silent and distant God. Even my bones suffer and cry out in the pain of unfulfilled hope and distant home. I put my hope in God for I will yet praise Him, my Savior and my God.
>
> —*Author's journal entry*

This suffering had all my attention, though it did not consume me. God allowed plenty of accelerant to be added to the fire, but He used the fire to burn up that which was not for my good. I was learning just how close He could be as He guided me through all this while I battled on.

Though these repeated attacks of the enemy were designed to keep me looking inward and to reduce my effectiveness for God, I found that the more prepared I was to wield God's Word and His truths, the less negative impact the resulting suffering had on my faith.

While it seems that God allows us to cry "Uncle!" in our pain, I have marveled at the breadth of His love as I trust Him more with my sufferings. It's as though I hold up my brokenness, like a prism, to Him as an offering and He shines His light through it, revealing a full spectrum and dispersion of the light of His love. Amazingly, something beautiful can be created out of something ugly.

Henri Nouwen writes:

> What are we then told to do with that pain, with that brokenness, that anguish, that agony that continually rises up in our heart? We are called to embrace it, to befriend it . . . and say that is my pain and I claim my pain as the way God is willing to show me his love.

Still on the hunt for more light to shine into my previously darkened thinking, I looked again to the wisdom of Paul:

> *But he said to me, "My grace is sufficient for you, for my power is made perfect in weakness." Therefore I will boast all the more gladly of my weaknesses, so that the power of Christ may rest upon me.*

For the sake of Christ, then, I am content with weaknesses, insults, hardships, persecutions, and calamities. For when I am weak, then I am strong.

2 Corinthians 12:9–10

Suffering can have ultimate meaning only in the context of God. He must be more valuable to me than my marriage, my health, my sufferings, and all my other mountains.

Chapter 10

Suffering and Character: Purposeful Pain

Strength in Joy, Beauty in Tears

God is always calling us into something we are not. He has greater things for us that we often cannot see, and it's rarely an easy stroll for us to get to where He is calling us. When we listen and follow that calling, we are going to experience pushback, feelings of hard pressing, a doubting and searching heart, and a spirit that might seem unsettled. Like a chick being pushed out of the nest by the mother bird, we are not sure what lies ahead for us.

We see or imagine the possibilities in front of us, and we want to fly; we might even have a dissatisfaction with our present state. Yet God can allow a very healthy amount of unrest to rise when we say "yes" to His leading.

No doubt you've noticed an unrest, an unresolved searching continuing in me. I often remind myself of all God's blessings and believe myself to be in His will, but God, for reasons I do not understand, allows this pressing to remain.

Over time, because this tension remains it can turn into an accusation that I must be doing something wrong, that God is not happy with me. This can be discouraging, but I have come to learn that this tension is a good sign, as it is a result of the Holy Spirit getting close to my flesh. There is a pressure as flesh responds to the discomfort of being close to holiness. It's not that something is wrong but that something is right! This can look and feel ugly, but it is our life being washed clean of our fleshly ways. It's a tension that likely will never go away as long as we are responding to His calling.

The enemy knows we stand in two worlds: as an alien in one and not yet present in the other. He will get into our business and sow confusion to discourage further trust in God.

Here is a journal entry I wrote well into my journey. Feel my searching heart, along with the hope that I still expressed:

> I feel a tension, a responsibility, a desire from God to stand for my wife and our marriage. This trial has a hold on me. My emotions are on the surface and tears flow. Yet Christ not only lives in me, He is also doing a good work. He puts a song in my heart, and He sustains me. He holds me close as He sanctifies me. His rod and staff comfort me.
>
> I have much inward joy, strength, and peace in my obedience and worship of Him. My thanks are always on my lips. Love, joy, and peace have increased in me, as evidenced by my service to others, my prayers, and my faith.
>
> Then *why* is my countenance so low and my hurt so potent? I return to God again and again for reprieve, strength, and hope. I accept this trial. I see His hand. So where is my outward joy?

Sorry, but this stuff is not for sissies.

We have covered a lot about suffering, but encouragement is on the way.

I now want to share some further wisdom I've gleaned and now treasure concerning this thing we call suffering. These are not simply bumper-sticker quips. They are a collection of bite-sized texts but Titan-sized truths, some from giants of faith, that have aroused me to hear the Holy Spirit speaking from His deep to my deep. I visit these truths for inspiration and confirmation in my life as I wrestle with my suffering.

I won't elaborate on all of these but encourage you to read Scripture, chew on it, and pray for God's message and wisdom for yourself:

- "We can ignore even pleasure. But pain insists upon being attended to. God whispers to us in our pleasures, speaks in our conscience, but shouts in our pains: it is his megaphone to rouse a deaf world."—C. S. Lewis, *The Problem of Pain*
- "Job never saw why he suffered, but he saw God, and that was enough."—Timothy Keller

- I found that looking for the why of suffering and for places to lay blame left me with unresolved feelings and deeper in depression. Do not search for causes of suffering—look instead for purpose. I found Isaiah 38:15–20 to be a great inspiration in my suffering as I shared in Hezekiah's search for meaning:

But what can I say? He has spoken to me, and he himself has done this.
I will walk humbly all my years because of this anguish of my soul.
Lord, by such things men live; and my spirit finds life in them too. You restored me to health and let me live.
Surely it was for my benefit that I suffered such anguish. In your love you kept me from the pit of destruction; you have put all my sins behind your back.
For the grave cannot praise you, death cannot sing your praise; those who go down to the pit cannot hope for your faithfulness.
The living, the living—they praise you, as I am doing today; fathers tell their children about your faithfulness.
The LORD will save me, and we will sing with stringed instruments all the days of our lives in the temple of the LORD.

Isaiah 38:15–20

- Over time, as God continued to demonstrate in my life His promise to use all things to always work for my good, I had to ask, "What is He doing in this trial?" This was not always clear or easy to decipher. It has become clearer to me that His greatest interest is in the condition of my soul and the resultant testimony of His providential leading in my journey, which He will then use to influence others in their own journeys. The healing of my marriage would only be a further extension of His grace.
- My suffering is not a detour. This alarming thought came to me: "Who's going to pray for my promised one if I don't stand for her? What if no one else is praying? What if I were being used to help break the chain of generational divorce and curses?"

Remember, I was once a prodigal. I now have street cred! I have empathy for her because I have lived with the churning inside when I turn from God's will and the resultant depression that just kind of hangs over my head, regardless of what I may admit to. Yes, I want a restored marriage, but more so, I want freedom for her!

Ha! My divorce, that I was once ashamed of and wished had never happened, God is using for His purposes! I was being asked to stand in the gap for my prodigal (Ezekiel 22:30, Isaiah 62:6–7).

- From a husband's perspective, read Ephesians 5:22–26. Doing Christian marriage right will cost men (me) more than it will cost women (her). That's not fair! This is hard for some of us to swallow. How much did Christ love the church? He loved her with a costly love. I need to embrace this and learn to live the principles behind it.

My restored wife, in our restored marriage, will never know the depth of prayers and tears that were expended for her, even if she reads this book. I must not only accept this but pursue forgetting what is behind and pressing on toward the goal. Why? First, I want to leave a path for her to find a way home by being careful and sensitive, protecting her from anything that would cause her to lose heart, to be overcome with guilt or grief, or to feel beholden to me. Second, take a moment and think about all the prayers that have gone up for each of us and the tears God shed as we each have willfully turned away and failed to trust. He is not waving all that in our faces.

If she is truly repentant and facing God, she will *know* and appreciate the depths of His sacrifice for her and the beauty of agape love inside a loving, sacrificial marriage.

- Two of the most powerful warriors are faith and time. How powerful! Just wait on God . . . and keep waiting in faith. God doesn't wear a watch. He's got this, but we need to wait for Him and allow Him to work His grace.
- If I really believed that God gave His own Son *unto death* to bring me to Himself, how could I give up when love becomes difficult? Just thinking about Jesus's death on the cross very quickly humbles me. My trials are truly light and momentary.
- My trials are an opportunity for me to know deep down that

my faith is genuine. I see my faith growing because I have been faithful with a little!
- God isn't bothered or hurt by my doubt. Doubt helps our faith and is not a sin. The opposite of faith is certainty, and where there is certainty there is no room for faith. Doubt is not the opposite of faith; it is one element of faith. Doubt is like an immunization—it will help fight off the virus of unbelief. I'll repeat—doubt always coexists with faith.
- If you don't have doubt, you're not doing this right, but we need to speak to our faith more than we speak to our doubt. Preach to yourself! No, really. Find some good fishing holes in Scripture and just soak in how faithful and good God is.
- "He has chosen not to heal me but to hold me. The more intense the pain, the closer His embrace. The greatest good suffering can do for me is to increase my capacity for God. Real satisfaction comes not in understanding God's motives but in understanding His character, in trusting in His promises, and in leaning on Him and resting in Him as the Sovereign who knows what He is doing and does all things well."—Joni Eareckson Tada, author and artist
- "We are not merely imperfect creatures who must be improved: we are, as Newman said, rebels who must lay down our arms. The first answer, then, to the question why our cure should be painful, is that to render back the will which we have so long claimed for our own, is in itself, wherever and however it is done, a grievous pain. . . . Hence the necessity to die daily: however often we think we have broken the rebellious self we shall still find it alive."—C. S. Lewis
- The closer I get to Jesus, the more evident my inadequacies become. Inadequacy causes me to seek affirmation. The only place to get the right kind of affirmation is from Jesus.
- When you don't understand, it doesn't mean that God has done something wrong; it just means that you don't understand. Big truth here. God's ways are not our ways. The Creator of the cosmos, who is always working for my good, is doing something different from the way I would have done it. Guess who needs to rethink their opinion?
- Patience and passion come from the same Latin root: *pati*. It means to suffer.

- The path of truth is often costly and lonely. Choose it anyway. Which path do I take? I mentioned the book of Ruth earlier. I encourage you to also read the Old Testament book of Hosea. We have a great deal in common with others who have walked in tough times. Their struggles and faithfulness will give you real encouragement to keep pursuing the will of God.
- "I feel you, tears. You make me want to quit. I know I will meet you several times each day. But I have work to do today and you will just have to go with me. I intend to take my bag of seeds and sow. If you come along then you will just have to wet the rows."—John Piper
- "If I knew any way of escape I would crawl through sewers to find it. But what is the good of telling you about my feelings? You know them already: they are the same as yours. I am not arguing that pain is not painful. Pain hurts. That is what the word means. I am only trying to show that the old Christian doctrine of being made "perfect through suffering" is not incredible. To prove it palatable is beyond my design."—C. S. Lewis, *The Problem of Pain*
- "When the pain and tears start all over again, maybe 2 days or 2 hours after the last attack—maybe it was not an imperfect healing or even the same wound. Maybe God is touching a new place in need of His Grace. Maybe yesterday's grief is now a scar ready to protect and God is working on another wound."—Unknown
- Here is a quote from A. W. Tozer that set me back in my seat. It is profound, almost enough to force me to shy away from contemplating it: "It is doubtful whether God can bless a man greatly until He has hurt him deeply." I'll let you ponder that.
- "The problem of reconciling human suffering with the existence of a God who loves, is only insoluble so long as we attach a trivial meaning to the word 'love,' and look on things as if man were the centre of them."—C. S. Lewis
- It is my studied reflection that it may be dangerous to make stopping your hurt a top priority. If you no longer feel anything, it's possible that you have shut down and are cutting yourself off spiritually and opening yourself to the enemy.
- Suffering is preparatory to sonship. Groaning is a prerequisite to glory (Romans 8).

- I doubt the hurt will ever really go away. I have been forgiven completely by God and fully restored in my relationship with Him. The enemy hates this and exploits any residual shame and tries to remind me of my past. He sometimes uses friends and family to subtly remind me that I am marked with a "D." He whispers, "Did God really forgive you for your divorce?" This is mostly a spiritual battle to try to render me ineffective. Unfortunately, sometimes it works. Worse yet, it can be a silent suffering.
- Like the surf's effect on a broken seashell, giving this hurt to God each day tumbles smooth the jagged edges of my shame and guilt. This allows the balm of His Word and grace to massage my heart and emotions. where only wise regret remains.

Here is where I was early on in my journey. I wrote a poem expressing my frame of mind based on Habakkuk 3:17–18:

Though aloneness intrudes when curtains are drawn, and laughter absent; only solitude to confide heart's pains, though the morning looks barren in this regard, though faith and hope have touched mountain peaks, still, I watch for a restoring hand to caress my cheek, though my tears have become like food,

yet I will rejoice in the Lord, I will be joyful in God my Savior.

—Author's personal version of Habakkuk 3:17–18

Though he slay me, yet will I hope in him.

Job 13:15

Chapter 11

Suffering and Hope: Unrequited Love

> Beloved, do not be surprised at the fiery trial when it comes upon you to test you, as though something strange were happening to you. But rejoice insofar as you share Christ's sufferings, that you may also rejoice and be glad when his glory is revealed.
>
> 1 Peter 4: 12-13 (ESV)

By now many of you have set yourself back in your chair, wondering about me. You might be thinking, "This guy has his life and identity wrapped up in this obsession with his ex-wife." You may be right. I've heard it before. People will tell me that God doesn't want me to suffer. It certainly doesn't look like the kind of suffering most of us can relate to. Yes, the initial divorce would rock most people, but to willingly subject oneself to "hanging on" smacks of desperation and not very 21st-century, me-centered thinking.

To love a prodigal is to live exposed, putting oneself out there, inviting attention with questionable odds of success, and living in subjugation to your calling. Sometimes my seemingly passive efforts and helpless feelings are palpable.

> Passivity is appropriate when we are being submissive to the will of God.

Hmm ... Who does that sound like?

> When they hurled their insults at him, he did not retaliate; when he suffered, he made no threats. Instead, he entrusted himself to him who judges justly.
>
> 1 Peter 2:23

Am I not sharing in the same suffering as Christ? Yes, Jesus was the unrequited lover in-chief!

God intimately knows the heartache of unrequited love. He experiences it every day as He intentionally pursues hearts that have turned cold, eyes that are searching for that almost satisfying sin, and tongues that speak only of self. Maybe we even lead Him on for a while, as we enjoy this new relationship with Him yet flee as soon as things get difficult.

God had unrequited love for Judah: "If she would turn back, I would accept her" (God, through the prophet Jeremiah, on Judah's infidelity).

Unrequited love opens us up to the pain of God experienced in the human heart of Jesus. Scripture—especially the Old Testament—is full of the imagery of God as the angry and rejected lover, but also the yearning, unrequited, and grieving lover: "*'Therefore my heart yearns for him; I have great compassion for him,' declares the* LORD" (Jeremiah 31:20). "*Or do you think Scripture says without reason that he jealously longs for the spirit he has caused to dwell in us*"? (James 4:5).

> "Meditating on the Old Testament has helped me to see God's long courtship of Israel as his lived experience of unrequited love."
>
> —Dr. Philippa Martyr, author and historian

For me, it takes deep contemplation and a sureness of the credibility of the Love Chapter to be sustained through a long season of unrequited love:

> *Love is patient, love is kind. It does not envy, it does not boast, it is not proud.*
> *It does not dishonor others, it is not self-seeking, it is not easily angered, it keeps no record of wrongs.*
> *Love does not delight in evil but rejoices with the truth.*
> *It always protects, always trusts, always hopes, always perseveres. Love never fails.*
>
> 1 Corinthians 13:4–8

> "The unrequited lover sees the beloved as perfected; as the finished product. This is how some have argued that God sees us outside of time,

which is why he can continue to love and forgive us with infinite patience. Perhaps unrequited love is a mercifully brief flash of insight into the love which God has for each one of us."

—Dr. Philippa Martyr

I have made a choice to love my prodigal, whether she deserves it or not, and to love her whether she returns my love or not.

"When we truly know the love of God, we are free to love others, regardless of their response, because we are secure in the love of the Father. The love of Jesus is the most fulfilling, the most rewarding, the most steadfast love that we can receive and share with others. When we are consumed by His love, it overflows into the hearts of everyone around us and there is no room for the ache of unrequited love, for we are safe in the love of our Savior."

—Jane Merson, The Ache of Unrequited Love

This kind of love is the basis of, and the influence on, the grace and empathy I have for my departed wife. Not an "I'm sorry you hurt your finger" type of love, but a "Father, forgive them, for they know not what they do" type of love.

I refer again to the book of Hosea. It is wonderfully hopeful and full of imagery of God's relentless, and even reckless, pursuit of our hearts. We learn that, when we participate in a quest for intimacy with another person, we are participating in a divine process. You can feel God's emotion and His pain of abandonment as Israel runs after other gods; the more He called, the further they ran. This is no aloof, detached deity. Rather, God's relationship with humankind involves emotional risk.

Hosea writes of God leading with compassion and, just as with the prodigal's father, setting things right by forgiving and not shaming, to lure the prodigal's heart back to Him. He will not let any of us wander too far from the relationship He has paid such a high price to establish in the first place, and He asks us to love the prodigal as He loves the Israelites. He asks us to "go show love to our wife again," to those estranged from God. I ask myself, "Does my love for my promised one look like this?"

Chapter 12

The Need to Have Need

It is better to go to the house of mourning than to go to the house of feasting, For that [day of death] is the end of every man, and the living will take it to heart and solemnly ponder its meaning.

Ecclesiastes 7:2 (AMP)

First Samuel 22 recounts the story of David hiding out in the caves of Adullum. It seems that some of his most painful and yet relatable psalms were written during this time. David didn't get the luxury of playing "church" in his cave, as he was in a very ugly period of life. God did not bring him there by accident, and David's journey did not end there. In his trials the religious was separated from the genuine. David's psalms show how he wrestled with his fears and with God's calling on his life. David became a witness, not a talker in those caves. Trials refined him into a warrior.

Like David, we all become pressed at some point, sometimes mightily so. We need the offending thing to go away; we need a less painful path so we can experience peace and happiness, or maybe just a full breath of adversity-free air in our lungs every now and then.

It is completely foreign to us to even entertain the suggestion that the greatest thing we have is what we don't have. *We need to have need.* It is in our trapped condition that God wants our intimacy with Him to grow deeper and sweeter. Will I, in the pressing, allow God to train and discipline me by removing pride and replacing it with humility, to change my heart to return grace and love rather than selfish impulses?

C. S. Lewis writes in *The Problem of Pain*:

> My own experience is something like this. I am progressing along the path of life in my ordinary contentedly fallen and godless con-

dition, absorbed in a merry meeting with my friends for the morrow or a bit of work that tickles my vanity to-day, a holiday or a new book, when suddenly a stab of abdominal pain that threatens serious disease, or a headline in the newspapers that threatens us all with destruction, sends this whole pack of cards tumbling down. At first I am overwhelmed, and all my little happinesses look like broken toys. Then, slowly, and reluctantly, bit by bit, I try to bring myself into the frame of mind that I should be in at all times. I remind myself that all these toys were never intended to possess my heart, that my true good is in another world and my only real treasure is Christ. And perhaps, by God's grace, I succeed, and for a day or two become a creature consciously dependent on God and drawing its strength from the right sources. But the moment the threat is withdrawn, my whole nature leaps back to the toys: I am even anxious, God forgive me, to banish from my mind the only thing that supported me under the threat because it is now associated with the misery of those few days. Thus, the terrible necessity of tribulation is only too clear. God has had me for but forty-eight hours and then only by dint of taking everything else away from me. Let Him but sheathe that sword for a moment and I behave like a puppy when the hated bath is over—I shake myself as dry as I can and race off to reacquire my comfortable dirtiness, if not in the nearest manure heap, at least in the nearest flower bed. and that is why tribulations cannot cease until God either sees us remade or sees that our remaking is now hopeless.

My most vocal unmet need has become a tremendous and effective focusing mechanism in my search for more understanding, meaning, and purpose in my journey. It has served to feed my faith and limit my unbelief as I hold up each verse that I read to see what God is saying to me in the mysteries of the sufferings I share in Him. Seemingly, everything goes through that filter, which keeps my heart very sensitive to what He is teaching me.

God will often answer our prayers and our needs in ways to further our faith by letting us experience the antithesis of what we are asking for. Think of the lame man healed by Jesus at the pool of Bethesda—in the morning when it is time to get up, who will know the love and the healing power of Jesus better than he? When the pain or need is great enough, we will drop all self-sufficiency and experience deep reservoirs of the knowledge of who He is.

If I ask God for more grace, I should expect answers that oppose my pride and humble me.

If I ask God for more faith, I should expect to be put into situations where my own answers do not satisfy, forcing me to look to Christ and His promises—I will be tested to walk by faith.

If I ask God for my joy to be made complete, I should expect my previous "joys" to suddenly not satisfy as much, so that I will search for the real joy in Christ.

If I ask God to make me a living sacrifice, I should expect to have my heart broken because the sacrifice acceptable to God is a broken spirit.

If I ask God to be my provider, I should expect that I am going to first have need so that I will be sure of what provision looks like!

> I'll never know the grace of God until
> I've known my own depravity.

The 42nd psalm speaks of deep calling to deep. I have run to that chapter many times as I cried out for the deep things of God to touch the deep needs inside me as I entered that most holy place—God's presence. It's in that place that depths can be found in God that I know nothing about: resources of great grace, comfort, and wisdom beyond my understanding. This place can be accessed through a special experience with God if we are wanting a stronger relationship with Him.

I'll admit to being a grace junkie, as I am always hunting for more. I believe that believers burn through more grace than sinners, and my pursuit is always seeking more of His grace. God never fails to meet me where I am at in my time of need. He lavishes grace on me, and it is sufficient!

Nevertheless, it's normal to be confused at times about what God is or is not doing. Our ongoing inadequacies and doubt will rattle the lion cage of our patience and sensibilities. We will roar in our own pity party or complain openly to others. As we suffer, in our unbelief we can fall into sin against God, or we might scream at Him in disappointment or anger. Our grieving sometimes turns to bitterness and our questions into accusations against Him. The cry of our flesh tries to take over.

We read in the psalms that even David was not above complaining in his need. But he had experienced tempering in his life; after falling many times he was able to take it to the proper place without a spirit of bitterness. In Psalm 42 we read David's anguished words to God from a heart that had an ingrained recognition that God is sovereign and good. David was not seeking relief from his circumstances—he was seeking more of God!

Looking again to the eleventh chapter of the book of John, the deliberate delay of Jesus to come and heal Lazarus on his deathbed did not seemingly meet the needs of His friends Mary and Martha (or Lazarus), especially considering this verse: *"Now Jesus loved Martha and her sister and Lazarus."* Because He loved them, he stayed two days longer where He was. This apparent contradiction is tough to handle because it is confusing to us. But it is a sign of His love. His delay will help us; it will not hurt us. We may be discouraged and confounded and may complain a bit because the seeming silence shows us how little of God we understand. In the wrestling with our needs we will learn, usually through repetition, that God always acts in perfect accord with what the situation demands.

Whatever we are traveling through—loneliness, loss, pain, sorrow—remember that these are disciplines; they are God's gifts to create need in us to drive us to His very heart so that He can increase our capacity for Him in the places we need. He will sharpen our sensitivities and understanding and will temper our spiritual lives so that they may become channels of his mercy to others, enabling us to bear fruit for his kingdom.

Learning to take all my cares to God has been a real breakthrough for me in my relationship to Him. I speak all my grievances—some would even call this raw discourse, though it is not disrespectful. He already knows! Isn't it another level of trust to be transparent and honest with someone and to risk revealing your heart with them? This pleases God. And it works in our human relationships as well.

> *You will keep him in perfect peace, whose mind is stayed on You, because he trusts in You.*
>
> Isaiah 26:3 NKJV

I experience a profound peace that comes from knowing that I am firmly held in Christ's hand when I call out to Him in my need. In

God's economy, grieving over our needs is permissible and valuable, as suffering causes us to search for answers. If we had all the answers, we would have no room for God, and the pain would still be there.

Just as taking all my cares to God creates a dependance in me on my faithful Father's grace, so does showing devotion to the very hopes He has instilled in me! I need His grace to help me live out my hope.

I spoke in chapter 3 of making an idol of my hope for a restored marriage. If I am not careful, this can become a very powerful, seemingly righteous and justified hope that can change my rudder just a bit and move my ship off course. This can happen if I begin to see God as a means to get my desires. Of course, I don't do this consciously, but I risk this when I don't trust His promise in Romans 5:5: "And hope does not disappoint us." My hope is in the One who gives me hope. Therefore, my hope for a rapturous marriage restoration is found only in my total trust in God for His will, His way, and His timing to be realized. My need is to trust Him in all things.

Knowing that my remarriage is not a right or a promise, I also give to Him my legitimate and very real desire to not remain single. The churchy phrase used here is "to put it on the altar." I am sacrificing on the altar my human desires and needs to my God, who *will not disappoint me!*

My hopes and desires don't disappear but do get reprioritized:

> *Take delight in the* Lord, *and he will give you the desires of your heart.*
>
> Psalm 37:4

In summary, we see that:
1. Our grieving in our need is permissible.
2. Our questioning of God in our need is acceptable.
3. Our unmet needs are meaningful catalysts in our lives.
4. Giving *all* our needs to God requires a need to trust God.

While we can appreciate the growth and maturation process in all of this, it is hard to live up to James's admonishment to "Consider it pure joy whenever we face trials of many kinds."

I am joyful *and* grateful that:
1. Christ suffered for me and suffers with me. I get to share in His suffering.

2. My greatest need is for the forgiveness of my sins (Colossians 1:13–14).
3. God's aim is to refine my faith, enlarge my holiness, save my soul, and that He would be glorified in me (1 Peter 1:7).
4. In my waiting, I am part of God's plan. He is using me. I am honored! I have joy in that.
5. In my need, I remember that waiting on the Lord is not a waste. My suffering and pain will not be victorious but will be purposeful.
6. My trials enable me to comfort and have compassion and mercy for others.
7. Satan is subordinate to God. He must have God's permission to attack us. If God can use it for our good, He may allow it into our lives.

"*May the name of the* L<small>ORD</small> *be praised*" (Job 1:21). These words are a protest against the tragedy of death that visited Job. I have tearfully stood over the grave of my disappointments and declared, "This is not over! One day Jesus is going to make this all right. Blessed be the name of the Lord."

Over time and through the trials, I finally found birthed in my spirit the realization that I am not in an ugly spot in my life. This is actually a very sweet place to be. I have relinquished control over my future and am experiencing a great deal of peace that God has for me. He is working all things out. When I consider my season of waiting, I know that I will experience God's will and peace either way this plays out. Either God will restore our relationship and marriage, and we will have a great testimony to our gracious and merciful God, or He has something else better for me in another direction. In that case, He will prepare my heart, my desires, and my prayers in advance, to turn this season of my life into something new. Goodness and mercy will follow me. See, I win either way!

This morning I awoke to an unsettled spirit. I prayed and wrestled with it for a while. I finally got a picture of a tree sending down roots with nothing apparent happening on the surface. A period of waiting was in the process; a building up of the soon-to-germinate, incorruptible seed of God was soon to come forth. Certainly not an original picture, but it brought a peace over me.

I got up, and my devotional was about the Spirit "brooding" over each of us. That word is used in some older translations of Genesis

1:2: God's Spirit was hovering or brooding over the earth. This is a picture of something building up and about to come forth, a birthing of something, a picture of a hen perched over her chicks.

The Holy Spirit is brooding over me. Though it has been a long process, there are things happening, I can sense it. The darkness, though present, is about to be overcome. Good things happen when the Holy Spirit is hunting for a place for His goodness to be manifested. My need is to *be* that place so I can have an encounter with our awesome God.

Chapter 13

Isaiah 54 vs. a Plumbing Predicament

Admittedly, you probably won't run into the above, borderline trivial analogy of perseverance anytime soon.

For a few days I had been wrestling in the book of Isaiah with the promises that God had given the Israelites and trying to draw out any personal promises, principles, and hope that I could. Of course, I read Isaiah 54:17: *"No weapon forged against you will prevail."*

On one of those days I was volunteering at a ministry, and I drew the short straw to fix a very old and clogged urinal in the men's room. Oh, thank you, Lord! A time to show my humility. Armed with a prayer, gloves, a plunger, a roto-rooter, and YouTube, I . . . dived in. It was a disgusting affair (several showers later on scarcely untraumatized me). The weapon of some foreign clog did indeed prevail. I was up to my elbows in it to prove that. Now, that restroom fixture was no longer usable in its current state. It was only an ugly wall ornament in need of fixing and a serious cleaning. It was of no use to anybody.

So, where does the plumbing story fit into my own? I often pray for dreams and visions from God right before I go to sleep. I am searching for deeper things from and about Him, so I ask for Him to speak to me while I sleep. The night after my unsuccessful roto-rooter party, I awoke at 2:00 AM thinking about the anatomy and plumbing of the urinal and the ways to defeat my foe. Soon—I'm guessing this was from God—I started thinking about the spiritual principles I could glean from my plumbing problem. I thought of the prodigal "clog" that

I had in my life and the fact that my life was not like a useless men's bathroom fixture. What to learn. . . ? Sometimes in life we do have weapons formed against us that do seem to prevail. We experience issues with health, death, relationships, financial lack, employment challenges, prodigals, and divorce. The list goes on. Of course, there are serious implications to all of these, and I am comforted by God's promises and care for us in all of them. But I have a major clog in my life that emanates its unholy smell all over the place in the here and now.

Hey, at times like this I just write down the stuff I think God has given me!

I cannot anticipate all the people or events my trials will impact. So, I choose to wait upon the Lord because He is God, and I am not. Will a nephew of mine read this book and be encouraged to share the good news of Jesus with a neighbor who will go on to become a preacher who will lead hundreds or thousands of souls to Christ? I sometimes see only the problem and the resulting mess. I must trust my prodigal clog issue to the One who sees it all.

I do see God at work in me, growing my patience, empathy, perspective, purpose, trust, appreciation, thankfulness, faith, hope, influence, encouragement, peace, wisdom, and strength. I resolve to continue to allow Him to help me walk a little more closely with Him each day.

I often run to my Daddy with open arms, on my knees with tears running down my face and crying out, "Will you please remove this weapon formed against me?" He says, "My grace is sufficient." Sometimes that is not what I want to hear, but it *is* what He wants me to learn. He then gives me enough grace to stand against it—usually, only enough for that day. I again cry out, "Give me a break. I don't want to fight this obstacle again tomorrow!" And this is what I hear:

> *Because of the* Lord's *great love, we are not consumed, for his compassions never fail.*
>
> Lamentations 3:22

We have been given the grace to stand. This is the reason we can't give up. God doesn't give us an extraordinary amount of grace to make life easy for us; instead, He gives us just enough so that in our weakness His power will be in us, ready for us to use. Grace is God's encouragement for us to stand against our enemy. He knows what's coming and doesn't want us to give up and miss it.

Once again, I taste and see that the Lord is good, and I learn to trust Him more.

Chapter 14

Am I on a Roller Coaster?

I just wanted to flatten the curve.

The term "flatten he curve" will forever be in our lexicon after COVID-19. It certainly applies to my current nonmedical condition.

It's going to happen. Some of life's moments are good and some are not. Add to the mix a couple of wounded hearts in a relationship, and the result can whiplash even the strongest. Sometimes I don't know if I am going up or coming down . . . or maybe even going backward.

And what's this about? The closer I get to God, the more hope and peace I have. And the more hope I have, the greater certainty I feel of an imminent, spontaneous, combustion-like victory and blessings, replete with trumpets blaring. I have that level of expectancy! When "spontaneous" takes on the speed of a slug, the fine line between peace and burden becomes a knife edge. It is tough to balance on. I start looking for answers to questions I am still trying to formulate.

Walking in God's calling is hard. He doesn't call us into easy things. Whatever your giant is will stretch you in ways you could never have believed possible. You might cry, you might scream, but for certain you will pray for your seemingly unbearable journey to end.

What can we do? God tells us what to do: come to Him every morning.

Lamentations 3:22–23 bears repeating: *"Because of the* Lord's *great love we are not consumed, for his compassions never fail. They are new every morning; great is your faithfulness."*

His mercies will never come to an end! Mercies can manifest in the form of encouragement, refreshing, revelation, or whatever it is that you are needing at that moment.

This is good news! But coming back to Him every morning looking for new mercies can be wearisome! Yes, it can. Often, I can't make it until the next morning. I need an infusion of mercy multiple times a day. Many days, I feel like I am starting at square one, having made no progress from the previous day.

Though His mercies are new every morning, on some days I don't consciously experience them. I don't "feel" their presence. On those days I must first fight a battle of faith versus feelings; then His encouragement flows to me. My journey thus far has taught me this: faith is not in what I feel. Trust is not in what I can touch. Hope is not in what I can hold. When I search for God each morning and honestly lay my hurts and doubts at His feet, He encourages me to stand for today. He encourages my hope to believe that with God all things are possible. I hunt in His Word, test it, question it, and then rest on it. I draw out more power by looking to the Lord and His strength and seeking His face always.

My journey is a testament to these encouraging truths. After all these trials and burdens pressing in on me for all these years, I would be an emotional wreck but for God's daily reorienting of my heart and soul. My problems don't disappear, but I learn to feed from His river of Living Water that picks me up and refreshes me for another day.

I don't want to say this too loudly for fear that God might hear, but I can tell you that His refreshing is so available and so encouraging to me *each day* that I believe it would be possible for me to live an entire life of such dependence amid my desperation. When I humbly open myself to it, it's that good.

Sometimes in my valley moments I find myself in a search for answers or direction that will land in my spirit and provide me some relief. The strengthening I need seems elusive. I am seeking, and yet God seems far away. Over time, I have realized that in my anxiousness, in my burden bearing, I am looking far ahead and doing mental gymnastics trying to solve problems that have not even presented themselves yet. I am futilely looking for answers to *all* the stuff swirling around in my head.

> *"Therefore, do not worry about tomorrow, for tomorrow will worry about itself. Each day has enough trouble of its own."*
> Matthew 6:34

Today's mercies are for today's troubles, and tomorrow's mercies are for tomorrow's troubles. The mercies He gives me each day are not for my whole mess! They are only for today, to get me through today. UGH! I was looking for more. From God's perspective—He is working to build my faith (that *is* what I had prayed for!). Read the story of the wandering Israelites in the book of Exodus miraculously receiving their bread each day. Coming to Him every day (or more often) is wearisome, but it does build patience, perseverance, strength, and self-control. It shows God that I have *faith*! Faith in His ability and willingness to provide it to me. The outflow of this is more rest and peace as He refreshes me in my trust.

What God has called me to do, He has graced me to do.

> *And God is able to make all grace abound to you, so that having all sufficiency in all things at all times, you may abound in every good work.*
> 2 Corinthians 9:8 (ESV)

I want to reference Hebrews 12:1 again for us to taste yet another chunk of God's encouragement:

> *Therefore, since we are surrounded by such a great cloud of witnesses, let us throw off everything that hinders and the sin that so easily entangles. And let us run with perseverance the race marked out for us.*

When I finish any of my endurance races, there are people at the finish line cheering me on. My legs are cramping, and my lungs are thundering. I want to quit! But not in the presence of so many witnesses.

I want to show well and finish strong. My pain is secondary as I near the finishers' chute.

We don't just have God on our side—we have the heroes of faith (Hebrews 11), the Hall of Famers cheering us on! The very men and women who have walked in great faith are not only an inspiring witness to us of God's great faithfulness but can be seen as surrounding us and encouraging us to finish strong.

Another truth came to me in my searching—God is a really good horticulturist. John 15 gives plenty of reason for the why and how of God's desire to grow in my life more and better fruit. Faith is fruit. So are love and joy. So, He introduced me to pruning. I already felt cut on and chopped enough. Just heal me! Ha! It's like pushups—it's not the first twenty that do a thing; it's the last five that the gain comes from. When I am finally in the right place and mindset to work with God and not against Him, He allows some pruning—not as a punishment but as a reward. He cuts away attitudes, pride, distrust, and unforgiveness that have no place in my life. He carefully prunes to continue to encourage more of what is already happening—producing more fruit of the Spirit.

Like waiting, pruning is not my go-to activity for fun!

If pruning isn't your thing, turn over in your Bible to Malachi 3. God also *"will sit as a refiner and purifier."* He will refine us in the furnace like gold and silver. *"Then the LORD will have men who will bring offerings in righteousness."* He is going to burn away that which is not of Him, *"'but do not fear me,' says the LORD Almighty."*

I have to stop myself occasionally to let this sink into every pore of my spirit—God is working many things to bring me into a trusting, secure, and growing relationship with Him. He cares about my hurts and feelings but is more interested in making me the kind of man who understands God's heart, sees with spiritual eyes, loves in difficult situations, and forgives when wronged. My feelings and wants are often contrary to God's purposes; therefore, something in me must get pruned or refined! I trust God and am so joyful that He loves me and sees so much potential in me.

Now, do I really think I am all the husband my returning prodigal spouse will ever need? Do I have all the edges rounded off, and will I always say and do the right things? No, but God is still at work in me. God is a better husband to my prodigal than I will ever be. He is the Father of prodigals. I want to learn from Him.

To fight back against the roller coaster feeling, I must remember that I am not fighting against flesh and blood. This is important:

How I see the battle is how I will fight the battle.

This is a spiritual battle. The enemy knows my weaknesses, but he also trembles at the knowledge of God, so I give God no rest in my prayers and in my faithful standing. Anything else I spend time pursuing in my own strength is unproductive.

By immersing myself in the book of Psalms, I join the fight. The encouragement of the psalms testifies how human hearts, weaned off fear, false security, empty comfort, status, pride, and money, can become effective warriors for the kingdom. The darkness is always trying to overcome the light, and I must fight every day by turning toward the light to allow it to push back the darkness of my fears and ignorance (Micah 7:8).

Healing is not in a straight line. There will be opposition.

You will likely learn that human heart healing is often not in a straight line, and you will feel the effects of this roller coaster ride. The enemy will soon follow us after some healing has taken place in our life and try to take it away from us. He tries to demoralize us in any way he can. Be ready for some opposition by being on guard and ready to take it to God to let Him oppose the enemy. This feeling of confusion is not from God. He is for us and wants our healing!

Know the truth. Seek the Holy Spirit for enablement. Cease striving. Know that God is at work. God promised to lay low our mountains, lift our valleys, and make the rough ground level. If that isn't anti-roller-coaster language, I don't know what is.

My part to counter the instability I am experiencing is to stay engaged in the spiritual aspect of this fight—to take my fight for reconciliation to God. Second Corinthians 5:20 tells me that I am Christ's ambassador, as though God were making His appeal through me. I shout in prayer to my prodigal, *"BE RECONCILED TO GOD!"*

Engaged means praying. I pray a lot, many times a day. Sometimes short and simple petitions and sometimes long. I cry routinely and fervently pray on my knees. My praying can often resemble a roller coaster as well—I can at times be in God's presence, enjoying the blessings of His Spirit and our joyous connection, while at other times it just hurts to pray.

In either the highs or lows of my feelings, I take what I have and where I am at to Him.

My pastor gave this advice when nothing else was working and the waves of doubt and despair seemed to keep breaking over me:

Just stare at Jesus.

That's better advice than it may sound:

> *Keep me as the apple of your eye; hide me in the shadow of your wings.*
>
> Psalm 17:8

The words "apple of your eye" are also found in Deuteronomy 32:10 (and other books), and this early reference might be the origin of this phrase. It means "little man of his eye," which refers to the tiny reflection of yourself you can see in the pupil of another person. If you could look into a child's eye and see your reflection in the dark of his pupil, you might be inclined to vow, "I can't harm this child; I see myself in his eyes."

Imagine God looking at you and seeing Himself in your eye. Thus, the phrase "apple of one's eye" developed to mean something treasured.

I'll leave this chapter with a story that really helped me to flatten the curve of my roller coaster feeling by setting my eyes and heart in a higher place:

In the book *Disappointment with God*, Philip Yancey writes about his friend, Douglas, who experienced a difficult trial. Douglas's wife contracted breast cancer, and then, during the crisis, while Douglas was driving down the street, a drunk driver swerved over the center line and smashed head on into his car.

Douglas received a massive blow to the head. His vision was affected and his ability to read was hindered. He could hardly walk down a flight of stairs without assistance.

Phillip interviewed Douglas to find out how he felt about his disappointment with God. Yancey writes (as shared by Shana Schutte in *When Life Isn't Fair,* Wisdom Hunters Devotionals):

Douglas was silent for what seemed like a long time. He stroked his peppery, gray beard and gazed off beyond my right shoulder. Finally he said, "To tell you the truth, Phillip, I didn't feel any disappointment with God.... The reason is this: I learned—first through my wife's illness and then especially through the accident, not to confuse God with life. I have learned to see beyond the physical reality in this world to the spiritual reality. We tend to think, "Life should be fair because God is fair." But God is not life. And if I confuse God with the physical reality of life by expecting constant health, for example, then I set myself up for a crashing disappointment. God's existence, even his love for me, does not depend upon my good health. Frankly, I've had more time and opportunity to work on my relationship with God during my impairment than before."

Douglas learned what is needed during trials—to believe without seeing. During our roller coaster trials, when God can feel absent, we must hold tight to the truth of who God says He is in His Word. This will hold us steadfast while everything around us is shaking.

Chapter 15

An Injustice, an Embrace, a Promise, and an Encouragement

*Whatever you have learned or received or heard from me,
or seen in me—put it into practice.
And the God of peace will be with you.*

Philippians 4:9

An Injustice

The prodigal son parable (as well as my story) can make us feel uncomfortable. It doesn't fit the normal construct we have about fairness and justice in personal relationships and in society. When a wrong has been committed, don't we sense a need for justice to help hold things together by keeping wrongs from turning into unpunished disorder?

In real life, for us to practice the sort of forgiveness displayed by the prodigal's father would not only appear naive but would seem to overstep personal boundaries of self-esteem. The love shown by the father is admirable, but our level of grace and compassion is more comfortable with the lump we get in our throat watching the pleas of starving children on TV.

How do we *really* react when a "sinner" returns to church post-sin expecting to be welcomed back into fellowship? Do we feel envy or bitterness when nothing good comes our way even though we've done everything right and the other guy, who has seemingly done nothing right, gets all the breaks? Do we differentiate between "good" Christians and "bad" Christians? Are we angry over an injustice that was done to us or resent that we are paying the price for someone else's wrong decisions? These are the prodigal's big brother attitudes that we all carry. These are human responses.

An Embrace

The prodigal father's welcome home embrace of his son was not behavior born of human feelings or even logic. The pardoning of all the hurts and tears caused by his son's offenses would not be what most of us would describe as fair or deserved. The father's stance wasn't "right" in the sense that we reactively feel a need to see evidence of a standard of justice—maybe a punishment or a process to "earn" back his father's love.

> Love and grace violate the very principle of fairness.

We feel that the older son should have gotten the party, not the younger one, but we are challenged to put those ideas of "fairness" and "deserving" aside because God's model of love and grace obliterates them. Grace is unfair. It means that we get something in our relationship with God that we don't deserve and that isn't justified. That's a paradigm shift in terms of how we view human relationships versus how God leads with love and grace.

Grace is the basis of the gospel message:
1. God made you and wants to have a relationship with you,
2. but your sin separates you from Him.
3. Jesus died for the punishment your sins deserved and rose again, giving you resurrected and eternal life,
4. so that, if you trust in Him for your salvation and turn from your sins, you will be forgiven, justified, and accepted, not because of your good deeds but freely by grace, and indwelt with His Spirit until you die and go to heaven.

That's why I have spoken so much of grace. It is a gift that transcends all logic. It is given for no reason except for God's love of each of us, to both good and bad people. It isn't a reward for our behavior. It's the glue that binds all Jesus's teaching together. Once you intentionally receive this gift, you grow and start to lead your life from a different perspective, and you instinctively invest yourself into others, modeling the same grace. A world filled with the gift of grace is a better world. People are given hope, forgiveness happens, relationships flourish, shame falls away, addictions disappear, and prodigals come home, not to deserved guilt but to grace.

> "Life happens for us, not to us. It's our job to find the grace in this and every moment of our lives —that's when life is truly magnificent."
>
> —*Tony Robbins*

A Promise

God has entered into a covenant with and has sworn a promise to, His children. His Holy name bears witness to the solemnity of it. At a marriage ceremony, before two become one flesh, we say before God: "With God as my witness, I take you as my covenant spouse, to have and to hold from this day forward, for better or worse, for richer or poorer, in sickness and in health, to love and to cherish, until we are parted by death. This is my solemn vow."

Wow, while walking in my faith journey, this marriage vow sounds just like God's promises to stand by me and protect me! God is gracing me, as a covenant marriage stander, with His heart to honor and protect the promises I have made—promises made without the demand of anything in return. For my prodigal spouse, away in the far country for a season, may I always hold true to them. "This is my solemn vow."

Because my prodigal and I are still one flesh under God, I have a platform to model Christ by dying to my need for justice and yielding myself to be used as a vessel in our restoration. God's Word promises in 1 Corinthians 7:14 that, by my allowing Him to first sanctify me, my prodigal spouse will be sanctified through me.

An Encouragement

Recently, I read a devotional based on 1 Peter 5:6–7:

> *Humble yourselves, therefore, under God's mighty hand, that he may lift you up in due time.*
> *Cast all your anxiety on him because he cares for you.*

The words, "that he may lift you up" (some Bible versions say "exalt you") caught my attention.

The Lord promises to come and lift us:
- He wants to lift up the discouraged.

> "The Lord upholds all who fall and lifts up all who are bowed down."
>
> Psalm 145:14

- He lifts up the hopeless.

> "He lifted me out of the slimy pit, out of the mud and mire; he set my feet on a rock and gave me a firm place to stand."
>
> Psalm 40:2

- He lifts up those who are facing opposition.

> "You exalted me above my foes."
>
> Psalm 18:48

- He lifts up those who are in trouble.

> "For in the day of trouble he will keep me safe in his dwelling; he will hide me in the shelter of his sacred tent and set me high upon a rock."
>
> Psalm 27:5

- He lifts up the humble.

> "The Lord sustains the humble."
>
> Psalm 147:6

- He lifts us up—we don't have to do it ourselves.

> "'Son of man, stand up on your feet and I will speak to you.' As he spoke, the Spirit came into me and raised me to my feet, and I heard him speaking to me.'"
>
> Ezekiel 2:1–2

Because I am confident in these truths, encouragement overflows from my certainty. Positionally, I am perfect with God. It's in my condition in my flesh that I know I will be going through a transition for the rest of my life. While the "in due time" promise from this verse above, candidly, leaves me wanting, I am certain He will not leave me in this condition. "In due time" will be in this life or in the world to come, and it will come at the proper, and God-ordained best, time. That's an encouragement that lifts me up!

You may be in a Saturday of your life as well, meaning in the day before Jesus's resurrection, when all seemed very bleak. Know the encouragement the Lord has for us:

- Revelation comes only in retrospect. Many things may be hidden from us at this point, but we must trust that "in due time" He will reveal all to us.

"*He reveals the deep thing of darkness and brings utter darkness into the light.*"

Job 12:22

- Prophesy to yourself and your situation. Find and speak encouraging Scriptures.

"*I remain confident of this: I will see the goodness of the Lord in the land of the living.*"

Psalm 27:13

"*For his anger lasts only a moment, but his favor lasts a lifetime; weeping may stay for the night, but rejoicing comes in the morning.*"

Psalm 30:5

- Stay the course. He remains faithful. Every single action God takes is sure and steady. Every word He speaks is always good and true.

"*For the word of the Lord is right and true; he is faithful in all he does.*"

Psalm 33:4

- Praise Him—Sunday is coming. God did not relinquish control at the cross. His plans for us are still in effect.

"*Let the message of Christ dwell among you richly as you teach and admonish one another with all wisdom through psalms, hymns, and songs from the Spirit, singing to God with gratitude in your hearts.*"

Colossians 3:16

Chapter 16

Areas of Growth and My Path for Progress

> Therefore, let us move beyond the elementary teachings about Christ and be taken forward to maturity, not laying again the foundation of repentance from acts that lead to death, and of faith in God.
>
> Hebrews 6:1

I have found that success in our relationship with our heavenly Father is not a formula. He treats each one of us as a unique person with our own characteristics, weaknesses, strengths, gifts, and purposes. He speaks to each of us differently and meets us where we are at along our unique path. No two people does He treat alike.

Looking back, I can see general areas of growth that God wanted to strengthen in me. For me to learn of these required being tuned in to His Word and His teaching; it took time studying, absorbing solid preaching, and praying, while allowing Him to prioritize and emphasize these things through our guide, the Holy Spirit.

It's like the old radios when we moved the tuning dial back and forth until we had dialed in the best signal. As we seek God and allow Him to "tune" us to His will, He will minimize the static and maximize our maturing process. Many of our needs in discipleship are common to all, and these can be great topics of Bible study and prayer. They are discussed in many venues and forums, so it is not hard to find information to start searching. The key to "tuning in" is the humbleness, openness, earnestness, and patience we apply to our searching. We do well to remember that this is a lifestyle—a process of building a relationship with God. Trying to figure out the Creator of the universe in three easy steps in three days would be frustrating and futile.

I listened and let God guide me in these areas where He showed me that I needed growth and encouragement:

1. Fall in love with the character of God.
2. Get rid of the sin in my life.
3. Seek Him and pray continuously.
4. Stand for Him.
5. Worship Him.
6. Be thankful to Him.
7. Serve others for Him.

I'll discuss each of these, below:

Fall in love with the character of God.

If I were to prioritize these areas of growth, this would be the first. Nothing will germinate in us if we fail to be awed by both God's vast power and His presence, as well as by His knowledge of the status of each of the very hairs on our head and His deep concern over the prayers on our lips.

Why and how God provoked me to look, contemplate, and then internalize His relentless goodness, I do not know. What I do know is this:

> "No one can come to me unless the Father who sent me draws them, and I will raise him up on the last day."
>
> John 6:44

His grace is poured out on all, inviting us to "taste" of Him and see. After tasting, only a fool would deny the attraction of such grace and love. I've learned that He is King, yet I've still experienced the love He has for even me. This encouraged the process of making Him the Lord of my life.

Get rid of the sin in my life.

> *If I had cherished sin in my heart, the Lord would not have listened;*
> *but God has surely listened and heard my voice in prayer.*
>
> Psalm 66:18–19

This is a journey unto itself. My repentance from sin is higher in God's priorities than the restoration of my marriage. Sin is a roadblock to God's working in my life because it allows my pride to say to Him, "I know better." Sin moves me away from the One who created and purposed me. Repentance turns me back to Him with a heart that says, "You know best."

Looking into myself to the roots and causes of my sin is humbling. It is not fun. Yet, because there is no condemnation and because God is patient, He helps me overcome my sin struggles. He lovingly shifts me from looking inward at my own self-centered desires, which over time define me to me, to seeking Him for identity and affirmation that confirms what my Spirit already knows me to be in Him! More concisely, He fills me with His Holy Spirit to crowd out that which he wants removed. While this can be an immediate change, in most cases this is a process over time.

Seek Him and pray continuously.

A couple of recent humorous, but instructive, "aha" moments I had with God: First, I was sitting by the water's edge of Crater Lake inside the dormant volcano at Crater Lake National Park in southern Oregon. While I was in wonderment at this beautiful park, I was alone and feeling it and was literally kicking rocks as a sign of my overly contemplative mood. I had my chin hanging low and rather absently-mindedly started to sing, "Show me your glory, show me your power." I looked up and very sheepishly acknowledged a wave of warm grace. God had put His arm around me and said, "Look up." Laid out before me was a carpet of the deepest blue water, encircled by a jagged ridge of snow-covered mountain peaks. It was overwhelmingly beautiful. I tasted His tender, generous and pursuing love, as He rewarded me for seeking His goodness. I said, "Thank you."

Also recently, I was walking along a fog-shrouded California beach not being able to see much of anything. I was again in one of my searching postures—looking in the sand and waves for any deep meaning I could extract. His message was right in front of me, but I was blinded by the heavy fog of my thoughts. Slightly wiser now, I chuckled to myself and asked God if He wanted me to trust Him even though I couldn't see, hear, or understand much of what was in front of me. I knew the answer but appreciated the gentle reminder.

These incidents reminded me of the words "There is beauty in what I can't comprehend" (from Brandon Lake's song "Too Good to

Not Believe"). God's love is beyond my comprehension, and to experience moments of the purity of it is beautiful.

Seeking God needs to include intercession for others as well—James 5:16 tells us to pray for each other. I have asked a few righteous people to keep knocking on heaven's door on my behalf, to keep my needs before our Father. I also seek godly counsel from them to check my path and progress.

I mentioned in an earlier chapter that I reread my journals and old sermon notes. This is something I don't want to gloss over. I receive tremendous encouragement and affirmation in looking back over the path I have walked. I am again illuminated by the beacons of wisdom that guided me through the valleys through which I have walked. Some of this stuff is sticking, and it is reaffirming to me the faithfulness of God. What a tremendous lived experience, as Isaiah 30:21 reveals:

Whether you turn to the right or to the left, your ears will hear a voice behind you, saying, "This is the way; walk in it."

During COVID, I joined our church's online Zoom prayer group for one-hour prayer sessions three times a week. We sought God for large and small needs. To pray out loud and regularly with five to ten others for over a year and a half gave me a great deal of experience to hear and practice unrehearsed and honest prayer. I gained great confidence as God grew my heart for receptivity to things of His heart.

I pray continually and give thanks in all circumstances. The persistent widow of the Gospel has nothing on me. I regularly knock—on anything as I pass by—and lift a prodigal prayer to my compassionate Daddy. I ask Him to send someone into her life to speak truth in love. I ask that, in the usual of her day, she would perceive the Holy Spirit reaching out to her, be it in the form of a billboard, a song, a commercial, a book, a look from her dog, or a persistent thought. I pray that I am discerning and right in my motives, and I am asking for whatever is best for my prodigal, not what's best for me.

My prayers represent my willingness, obedience, and faith to give God my five loaves of bread and two fish (Matthew 14), as I believe in His power of provision above all I could ask or think. He hears my same prayer many times over. I know He is at work, and I let Him know that my hope is still in Him, no matter how many times I come to Him.

I don't pray wimpy, rote prayers. I have a need, and I have a Father who can fix it and cares about me. As an adopted son by His choosing, I walk boldly into His throne room and call on His name and remind Him of His promises—respectfully, of course. My prayers are not sophisticated—I would be embarrassed to hear some of them played back. I probably sound like I am lost in the fog! But they are raw and childlike as I search for His promises and truth.

> *You will seek me and find me, when you seek me with all your heart.*
>
> Jeremiah 29:13 (ESV)

The good news is that I am not in a fog. His promises steady my feet as He guides me. That is His namesake, His style, His signature. He is a good, good Father who loves me, waits for me, and works to enlarge my holiness. I may think I am all alone, walking in the valley of the shadow of death, yet I know that I have a Daddy who bends down to listen to me, provides me protection under His wing, is my strong tower, is shining a light on my path, and goes before me to make my crooked paths straight.

My prayers help me to "tune" God in as I am being open and introspective with Him. This is a good check in terms of growth in my faith and the way His resurrection power is being reflected in me and through me. I have learned that His power is not in how I feel but in how I live.

Stand for Him.

> *Therefore, my dear brothers and sisters, stand firm. Let nothing move you. Always give yourselves fully to the work of the Lord, because you know that your labor in the Lord is not in vain.*
>
> 1 Corinthians 15:58

I have resolved to wait on God. I stand for His righteousness for His namesake. Though I don't always know what He is doing, or if He is going in a different direction from what I want, I will still follow Him. Sometimes I must repeat, "Jesus, I trust in you! Jesus, I trust in you!" I do trust Him. I have resolved to do what God has called me to do and to love Him more than my need to have a restored marriage.

Standing for God means that we pursue what He desires in a situation—not what we want. I have changed my approach to my prayers for my promised one to reflect more of God's bottomless grace—I pray blessings great and rich for her. I want her eyes to be drawn to the deep grace of Jesus. Give her blessings, Lord; grant her more grace!

Why do I bless her? First, because I love her, but I know God won't bless her until she is bless-able—walking in light and truth. If we are not in a right relationship with God, discipline and chastisement must happen before we can be blessed. He must prepare our heart to receive His blessings; we must first have our *Kairos* moment, a time when we "come to our senses."

Blessing her also lessens in me any desire for bitterness and retaliation. Bless her, Lord, in all things. I used to pray for confusion and pain so she would be motivated to turn back. Now, God may use pain and shaking, but He leads with a Galatians 6:9 spirit, offering grace with tender whispers. We read in the book of Hosea how God is going to allure an unrepentant Israel by leading her into the desert and speaking tenderly to her. God leads with love!

I am also learning to stand for God by practicing a principle of lifting my prodigal (and others) by speaking Scripture and destiny into her life. His Word declares each and all the following:

> *My promised one has the mind of Christ; she is a chosen people, a royal priesthood, a holy nation, God's special possession; she is the head, not the tail, above and not beneath; she is delivered from the power of darkness; greater is He who is in her than he who is in the world; she is released from the spirit of fear; no weapon formed against her shall prosper; the peace of God, which surpasses all comprehension, guards her heart and mind in Christ Jesus; and I know that He who has begun a good work in her will complete it.*

Standing for God means acknowledging that His ways are better—in all circumstances. We need to turn (repentance) from what we want and learn to follow (obedience) His better way.

What is the speed of light? About 186,000 miles per second. What is the speed of darkness? Darkness flees just ahead of light at the same speed. We need only to turn on the light of the gospel of Jesus Christ, and the darkness will always flee. Darkness will not linger; it will not overpower the Light; it will not become less dark. No, it will be overcome by the Light. To stand for the things of God, our lives need to reflect His light. To counter the darkness, we need to respond in the opposite spirit, the Spirit of Light, and speak out: "His Word declares . . . !"

We as Christians all love and quote John 3:16. It is a great promise, and this gift from God is not only an encouragement but a declaration of our very salvation. But it is only part of the story of our relationship with Him. First John 3:16 continues with the validation of whether John 3:16 is making any difference in our lives—Are we laying our lives down for our brothers? Are we loving with actions? John 3:16 is a blessing, and 1 John 3:16 is an experience of obedience and sacrifice.

Jesus showed us His rugged love by making a stand on a rugged cross—a love with sacrifice! He is asking from us a sacrificial love toward others as well that is:
- strong enough to face evil,
- tenacious enough to do good,
- courageous enough to enforce consequences,
- sturdy enough to be patient,
- resilient enough to forgive, and
- trusting enough to pray boldly.

Yes, I feel the oppression and the war of weariness from the enemy in my stand for my prodigal, but I also experience His light; I have glimpsed the train of His robe filling the temple, which compels me to say, "Here am I. Send me. Use me for your good." What if I were to quit standing? Wouldn't I then become a prodigal myself in search of my own pleasures? To have the privilege to walk in this kind of faith and sacrifice and to share in His ultimate victory makes my trial pretty awesome!

Worship Him.

Worship is many things. All my actions listed in this chapter are acts of worship. A simple definition of worship: being faithful in a thousand small acts of obedience. I think the most precious form of worship is the soul that has been crushed but chooses to cling to the Lord and follow Him anyway.

For this discussion I am referring to both corporate and private exultation of our Lord and Creator. Sometimes that looks like singing with hands in the air, while at other times it means quietly meditating and listening for God's small, still voice.

In just the last few years all my worship has become much more expressive and animated. I am easily stirred to lift holy hands in song, to pray, and to dance. This becomes a transparent mixture of passion and urgency as I seek more of Him in hope and thank Him in joy. Often the tears flow, and I really don't know if I am happy or sad. It doesn't matter. I am in His presence.

When I am happiest, I worship. When I am most disappointed, I worship. While I wait, I worship. I follow King David's lead here. Not only does worship help in the spiritual realms, but it also connects my heart with God's heart. He inhabits my praises. He put a thirst in me to worship. It's like standing at the edge of the Grand Canyon in reverent awe—I can move a couple of feet or turn just a bit and get a new look at the unfolding of His grace and unparalleled beauty.

Worship knocks the enemy out of the picture as it ushers us into God's holy presence. Worship centers our consciousness on the able One, subdues the trembling heart, lifts our countenance, and redirects our wandering soul, all while displacing hopelessness with hope. Worship is releasing the pent-up pressure of our desire to reunite our soul with its Creator.

Be Thankful to Him.

In the middle of life's struggles, it is easy to look at our problems and miss perceiving God's gifts. Being thankful with an appreciative heart is a habit I have long tried to feed. Regardless of my everyday circumstances, my blessings are plentiful. Small things can quietly pass me if I am not careful, but remembering a forgotten detail, finding an open parking spot, recovering lost keys, getting a good night's sleep, or hearing a bird's chirp has often caused me to pause and say, "Thank you"; sometimes I exclaim that for no reason other than that I *am* thankful.

I even go so far as to build spiritual altars at the physical places where I have met with God—honoring memories of deep encounters.

I have such designated locations scattered around the country; they await my return to direct my heart back to that same intimate encounter I had with Him at our previous meeting. I get to relive His presence, His provision, and His promises. And then I always thank Him.

You are probably familiar with rock cairns, piles of rocks helping to mark the path of a trail. In my hiking I often see them as altars that prompt thoughts of thankfulness.

> *Moses built an altar and named it The Lord is My Banner.*
> Exodus 17:15 (NASB)

I believe that thankfulness secures our blessings. God's grace may shine upon me differently tomorrow, but I let Him know that I appreciate Him as my provider, my protector, and my sustainer.

I believe that gratitude turns whatever you have into enough. Your heart becomes content with what you have when you realize *all* that you have.

I regularly thank God for my prodigal. She is a part of something that is causing God to powerfully demonstrate His love for us, bringing our lives into step with Him. That prevails over the pain!

> *Give thanks in all circumstances; for this is God's will for you in Christ Jesus.*
> 1 Thessalonians 5:18

Serve others for Him.

> "The more time you spend thinking about yourself, the more suffering you will experience."
> —*Archbishop Desmond Tutu*

Currently, I'm on my "Seek, Serve, and See tour" as God leads. Nearly three years ago I left home behind, alone yet wanting to be faithful to our (her and my) plans to travel full-time and serve God. I have ample time to seek Him and enjoy a growing relationship with Him. The glue that helps hold my days and mission together is my serving in different ministries, each for several months at a time. I can be a part of a community, worshiping and working with many different believers. I am being blessed and blessing them as we build the kingdom together. My seeing is the traveling around the country in my RV. I have opportunities to witness many awesome sights in our country. I regularly get my fix of hiking in some very beautiful places. This has been a journey with a purpose.

When I serve, my self-esteem grows. But without serving others, I can become self-centered in my cares, desires, anxieties, and even in nursing my wounds. Caring for others for Christ's sake is a beautiful expression of a life on purpose for God. Your own application of service to others will look different, based on your season and giftedness. I have found that there are many, many opportunities out there to become a part of to serve His kingdom.

Chapter 17

Hope and Healing

*Therefore, if anyone is in Christ, the new creation has come:
The old has gone, the new is here!*

2 Corinthians 5:17

In my journey through my valley, I have placed my wounded heart in the King's hand, looking for His healing. I received much more than that—a refining in the furnace of suffering.

In my valley I have encountered the Lily of the Valley, Jesus, the purifier of heart and soul and the star of this show. This journey is not primarily about a prodigal or about my prayers and pain. It is about Jesus. It is about what He is doing in and through me—how he wants to forge in me a faith, a maturing of character, and a knowledge of the hope to which He has called me.

I owe praise and honor to Him for the riches of His glorious inheritance and for the incomparably great power that is also producing these other gifts in me:

1. Peace and Joy.
2. Wisdom.
3. Faith and Hope.
4. Purpose.
5. Truth.
6. Other Minded.

I'll discuss each of these, below:

Peace and Joy

I hear the claim that, if we could go back in time, do things differently, and correct our mistakes, we would experience life in an expanded, more joyful way. Do I have regrets? Yes, I do. Would I change some things? Of course. However, I have learned that no one has a straight-line progression to peace and joy. We all get a bit of craziness mixed in. That is the path from sinner to saint. It's part of our human experience.

> "The joy of the future and God's plans for my life aren't worth sacrificing for a past I can't change."
>
> —*Shana Schutte,* Wisdom Hunters

In our searching we can learn of our true identity and find that we can hold firm to this truth: God is interested in our new, not in our old. Each one of us is a new creation if we are in Christ. True peace and joy come not from our old identity but are a result of our new spirit being brought into right relationship with our Creator. This inward alignment also exhibits itself as an outward and confirming joy.

> *But the fruit of the Spirit is love, joy, peace, patience, kindness, goodness, faithfulness, gentleness, self-control.*
>
> Galatians 5:22-23 (ESV)

The fruit that the Spirit produced in the heart of the believer includes peace and joy. We can make our stands and fight our battles because we have heaven's perspective and God's promises for His best outcomes. We also can remember our past experiences of trusting Him—we saw His goodness, we didn't get hurt, and He grew our faith, which resulted in peace and serious joy.

In the middle of my battle, this hasn't always been an easy path for me. My shield of faith has been a very present reality, but it is as though I have had to stay hunkered down behind it for its continued protection. I have not often been able to stretch out, fill my lungs, shout out my joy, and bask in my peace. Hence, I have this reservoir of joy in me that has not been fully tapped and released because of the battle that continues around me. My joy wants to blossom and cry out on the mountaintops, but for now it serves as an intimate and vital sustenance that feeds me.

Happiness is dependent on external happenings. Joy is an inward connection to the source of all joy (God) and to a firm foundation of truth (God's) that anchors our hope. When we befriend untruths, our hope is subject to confusion and thus becomes weakened.

In Paul's words in Romans 15:13

> *May the God of hope fill you with all joy and peace as you trust in Him, so that you may overflow with hope by the power of the Holy Spirit.*

It's God's job to give joy. Our job is to get in the way of joy and put ourselves in a place to receive it. He has a never-ending, overflowing spring of joy for us that flows from our future, our eternal salvation, back to our present. Faith sits us in the middle of that spring.

If we look around, we see that there is delight and beauty to be encountered in our daily lives. Our world is never void of the great reality of God and His love for us. Our hunting for that helps us to resist the temptation to look into the future with fear and anxiety, as well as to look back to the past with regret. Instead, we are to be in the present and abide in Him in peace and joy.

Without knowing whether my prodigal comes home or not, would I go through this journey again? Fortunately, that is an abstract enough question that I don't have to answer it. But I will state, with certainty, that I am content and grateful in my circumstances. I am even joyful! This walk has been a precious gift—I would not want to risk missing out on the goodness He is now giving to me. The God of our universe is bending down to hear my cries and doing so with great care to not break this bruised reed; He is breathing healing and life-affirming peace into this old soul. This I know: that peace is a promise He keeps.

In my circumstances, despite my affections for all my investments in my carefully reasoned plans, my logical fears, and my unrecognized ignorance, I opened the door, allowing God to prove His promises to me. I put my trust in Him for my hope and future because I believe He will never stop doing good and will make my joy complete.

Folks, as I have always told my kids, "It don't get any better than this!"

Wisdom

"When you're young, life feels like an ever-expanding horizon, with infinite time and options at your disposal. Yet a day will come when that horizon reaches its expansive limit, and then you increasingly will feel the narrowing reality and fleeting nature of your life. This happens to all of us, yet the wise are able to see it coming long before it arrives!"

—Anonymous

Wisdom is a benefit of walking with God.

> *So teach us to number our days that we may get a heart of wisdom.*
>
> Psalm 90:12 (ESV)

Most of us try to push the limits of our lives as we look for greener pastures, distractions from the root issues of our reoccurring problems, or just new thrills in life. The risk in this is that it breaks us from the continuity of our story and learned pathways. We then are unable to anticipate outcomes, and we may make many of the same mistakes over again. The finite nature of life means that we have a limited number of days to acquire wisdom. The more we embrace this reality, the more we grow in wisdom, which layers into our soul, giving birth to a wise and peaceful heart.

A growing, God-fashioned wise and peaceful heart has been a precious asset that is serving me well in my current journey by not allowing the rise of resentment, anger, unforgiveness, or bitterness. My own prodigal years were in part due to my insecurities from a real or perceived lack of respect and affirmation—a sense of abandonment. Add to that this more recent, very real abandonment that I have experienced, and I could have become too fast a car on a winding mountain road. I thank God for His promise in Psalm 37:23–24:

> *The Lord makes firm the steps of the one who delights in him; though he may stumble,*
> *he will not fall, for the Lord upholds him with his hand.*

Yes, rogue thoughts of exacting justice, wanting validation, pitying my poor position, wanting to be proved right, or feeling unloved can do a drive-by in my head occasionally. These are fleeting thoughts at best and rarely turn into sin. I know what God's promises are and that they are for me, so I hold fast to them.

This is not just a work on my own part to overcome such thoughts. It is also the work of the Holy Spirit as I pursue Him and align myself with His desires:

> *Those who live according to the flesh have their minds set on what the flesh desires; but those who live in accordance with the Spirit have their minds set on what the Spirit desires.*
>
> Romans 8:5

I am still learning and putting into practice the truth that this journey is about Him. It truly isn't about me; I'm doing this for the glory of God.

Yet, wisdom wants to go further by teaching us that "knowing God" should be followed by "growing in God." In Isaiah 55:8 in The Message: God says, "*'I don't think the way you think. The way you work isn't the way I work.'*"

All our senses, feelings, and flesh seek miracles; we long to hear God's audible voice, see the Red Sea split, touch and eat manna from heaven, or feel a wind rushing in to blow away our cares.

> *He made known his ways unto Moses, his acts unto the children of Israel.*
>
> Psalm 103:7 (KJV)

God revealed His acts. The children of Israel saw the miracles and had knowledge, but Moses knew the ways of God. Because he knew why God had done those things, he gained wisdom. The goal for us is not just acquiring knowledge of God but learning wisdom from having the mind of Christ.

Faith and Hope

God promises us that He will protect our faith because it is important to Him. That's the good part. He will also exercise our faith in different ways to keep it strong. That can be the scary part.

Before bed I usually pray for God's protection during my sleep from the enemy's lies and distortions and from his sowing seeds of confusion into me. My prayers have largely been effective, but not always. I sometimes become unsettled after having prayed this prayer and then experiencing a disturbing dream. I have had different dreams of reconciliation with my prodigal, only to have her still displaying "far country" words and attitudes. I have awakened at such times to confusion and hurt! "What was that about, God?"

I have concluded that God does allow some space for Satan to operate in my life to allow me an opportunity to exercise and demonstrate my faith! Huh? Yes. God has matured me to the point that I can fight back and extinguish the arrows of the enemy by being properly armored in Him. He is my shield and protector, and I am using His truth and power to overcome stuff that used to diminish my peace, time, and energy in my anguish! So, now I also pray for my faith to be strengthened so that I will be ready to stand when needed. I pray for a faith more precious than gold!

I am excited and humbled about being used by God even though He didn't find me faithful—nor did I earn this. Still, He judged me faithful (1 Timothy 1:12), regarded me as faithful, and esteemed me faithful. Grace!

I am learning to come to God like a child. I try not to lay it out and figure it all out for Him. My desired approach is to reflect how I would approach my earthly father: "My balloon popped, Daddy. Please fix it." Now, I am trusting Lord Daddy to work it out for my good.

Having a stronger faith helps me to see more clearly and to appreciate and celebrate the spiritual growth I am walking through. In their forty-year wait, Caleb and Joshua learned a deep faithfulness in God's provision. They experienced a daily strengthening that cemented a trust in their calling. And when the time came, they were ready to be used by God to deliver on His great promises.

> God is transforming me from a wounded spouse
> to a warrior spouse.

Purpose

King David had a résumé that few of us could match—murder and adultery included. Yet in his humbleness and contriteness and his having been given the amazing grace of God, David discovered and served out his purpose in his moment in history. His writings in the songbook of Psalms teach us proper priorities in the praise and worship of our Lord and King, Jesus. David's honest poetry exposes our hopeless weaknesses when he sings for all our hearts as we search for meaning and purpose in our lives.

Our ultimate purpose is to glorify God. David. in his very flawed state, found that purpose.

> *I cry out to God Most High, to God who fulfills his purpose for me.*
>
> Psalm 57:2 (ESV)

My journey has similarities to David's journey. Through God's grace and patience, I am discovering purpose in my life. Though sometimes I grow weary of looking down the road and watering my seeds of hope, I remain steadfast, while voicing David's cry:

> *In the morning, LORD, you hear my voice; in the morning I lay my requests before you and wait expectantly.*
>
> Psalm 5:3

Each of us has an important assignment within our own journey given to us by God. Every assignment has value and purpose. We might not even see the significance or impact of our assignment, and again, most likely neither will our family or friends. God looks through the lens of eternity and depends on us to trust Him and His promises to operate in faith—faith in His desire to set us apart from birth for our assignment and for His grace to complete it.

I have a strong hope to follow the same path to restoration that the prodigal son's family was graced with. However, my ultimate victory is found in Christ and the direction that He may lead. I won't resent the refining He is bringing me through, for I have become convinced that my discipline, training, and growing in character, by God's grace, are my ticket to learn my ministry. Somewhere, sometime, God is going to use the fruits of this journey in a ministry opportunity that will bring help, hope, and healing to some of His children. This refining is the process of empowering and giving me authority in it.

Truth

> *I am a sojourner on the earth; hide not your commandments from me!*
>
> Psalm 119:19 (ESV)

C. S. Lewis describes how God refreshes us along life's journey of suffering:

> The settled happiness and security which we all desire, God withholds from us by the very nature of the world: but joy, pleasure, and merriment, He has scattered broadcast. We are never safe, but we have plenty of fun, and some ecstasy. It is not hard to see why. The security we crave would teach us to rest our hearts in this world and pose an obstacle to our return to God: a few moments of happy love, a landscape, a symphony, a merry meeting with our friends, a bathe or a football match, have no such tendency. Our Father refreshes us on the journey with some pleasant inns, but will not encourage us to mistake them for home.

My wake-up and out-the-door inclination every morning could look to befriend the world and make myself a home here. Yet, I am by rebirth a sojourner, a stranger here. I must stop and incline my head and heart and serve a different appetite, a craving that does not tantalize my senses but calls out to me in a gentle whisper. His love causes me to listen in faith because His promises are greater than the intrigues of this world.

Our ability to rely on worldly truths will get us only so far. These are some of the things we are exposed to every day, some of which each of us has given voice to—but these are things Jesus *never* said:
- Listen to your heart.
- Be true to yourself.
- Trust your gut.
- Feel good about who you are.
- Happiness is what matters.
- Just be a good person.

What Jesus actually said:

> "If anyone would come after me, let him deny himself and takeup his cross daily and follow me."
> Luke 9:23 (ESV)

In my journey of transformation, I sometimes make friends with my feelings and embrace a sorry state of hopelessness. Thankfully, I have an ever-present shield given to me to extinguish the scheming and discouraging arrows of the enemy.

There are two truths that are protected from the enemy that give me great strength. First, I have *hope!* Against all odds, my hope is more palpable than ever before. Not a superficial hope with my eyes squeezed tight, but a sure hope birthed and fed by God. After enduring this long and heavy wait, the fact that I am still this hopeful is an unarguable miracle to me. Second—I cannot otherwise explain why I don't have my therapist on speed-dial—God restores my soul each and every day. The hungry lion seeks his fill, yet I stand. I am not consumed!

We need God's presence in our life because the truth of our condition and the truth of God's provision are married by the Holy Spirit into an able and reliable teacher and guide for us. He guides us into all truth. We have the indwelling of the Holy Spirit so that, when we run out of our ability, we are well positioned to receive a fresh filling from Him. We may not know what to do, but the Holy Spirit does.

Other Minded

As I love and serve others for God, I become "other minded." It is important to see ourselves the way Jesus sees us so we can be that for other people.

"Instead of cutting down a life lacking fruit, we are called to lift his sagging self and nurture him back to health. Regardless of the reasons for ones' inability to be a fruitful follower of Jesus, sometimes it requires removing the cares of this world . . . to cultivate forgiveness and irrigate hope. A life so beat down by bad choices (personal or provoked by another), desperately needs a safe environment to recover and be restored. If we were suffering difficult days, we would want mercy . . . a second chance. Grace does this . . . even third, fourth, or fifth chances. Lift up another wilting life in prayer and with practical help so he is able to forgive his shame and seek to get right with God over the guilt of his sins. Second chances give life to lives toying with giving up."—Boyd Bailey, Wisdom Hunters Devotionals

I'm reminded of my twin son and daughter when they were young. My son was very competitive and was always challenging his sister to anything physical. Usually he won and would declare, "I won, I won!" When she did come out on top, she was equally gleeful but shouted, "We won, we won!" Mom and Dad were humbled by her childlike approach to others. Unfortunately, most of us pursue life with an "I" attitude. A heart that seeks the "we" in life pleases the Father.

Chapter 18

Thoughts of My Ongoing Journey

"For you will certainly carry out God's purpose, however you act, but it makes a difference to you whether you serve like Judas or like John."

—C. S. Lewis

One of the prayers I voice often for my prodigal I wrote based on Ephesians 1:17–18: "I keep asking that the God of my Lord, Jesus Christ, my glorious Father, may give _____ the spirit of wisdom and revelation, so that she may know you better. I pray also that the eyes of her heart may be enlightened in order that she may know the hope to which you have called her, the riches of your glorious inheritance in the saints, and your incomparably great power for us who believe. In Jesus's name I pray."

My journey is not over. It's not over because of what I want or what I think is due me but based on God's continued and faithful leading. Everything in this journey that I have experienced has been given to me to use for His glory. My hope has grown into a true and mature hope:

> In my family we do second chances, we do grace, we do real, we do prayers, we do mistakes, we do I'm sorry, we do forgiveness really well, we do hugs, we do love, we do family to death do us part. We don't do shame.

Everyone would agree that this is good advice to live by, and I aim to be faithful to it. But not everyone is in a place where they can relate to the road I have traveled to this point. I was a doubter not so long ago.

I am reminded of one of my favorite Bible stories, told in the Gospels of Matthew and Mark. After witnessing the miraculous feeding of the five thousand, the disciples were wrestling with what they had just seen and experienced. Jesus then told them to get into a boat and to "go on ahead "of Him to the other side of the Sea of Galilee. After some time they had not gotten far, for the wind was against them, and they were straining at the oars before Jesus walked on the water, to their rescue and amazement.

It could be argued that I have not traveled far from the point from which I started this journey of mine. Certainly, it feels like the wind and waves are against me, and I am straining at the oars. But I do know that I have been asked to get into my boat and to go on ahead of Him. I believe He will meet me, and if you have walked these pages with me, you have seen God at work. To read this is encouraging; to live it is profound.

> *Blessed are those whose strength is in you, whose hearts are set on pilgrimage.*
>
> Psalm 84:5

If you are at the beginning or in the middle of your own profound journey, and you feel like there's something next, some unfinished business, that's because there is something next. Just as creation is groaning, your groaning is from a growing hope and an anticipation of your future sonship (Romans 8). Your faith is being fueled and is expanding from a believing faith to a receiving faith. Not only do we believe God is able to change hearts and minds, but we also stand, secure that we are a worthy and acceptable candidate for His pursuing goodness. In due time you, too, will be able to say, "for thou art with me." To diligently hunt for His best for you, you will experience delivered promises and miraculous miracles that will refine your faith, more precious than silver or gold.

Don't be surprised to learn that standers are, for the most part, an unheard from group, back there in the shadows. Standing is countercultural, and eyebrows are even raised by some church members over this idea. Society does not discourage divorce; it is nearly as natural as getting married. Prioritizing your own wellbeing above that of others and viewing relationships as a means to affirm yourself are more the mainstream. Friends and family members can often unwittingly pressure you with the same rationale.

If you have your eyes and heart on things above, these distractions will not matter much to you. Let me assure you that there are a lot of standers out there in some phase of their own journey.

Probably, in all cases, the stander is wrestling with some level of doubt that God can or will bring a restoration. A fully restored marriage is not a 100% guarantee. With all these issues, as well as some level of shame swirling around in the mind of an already distraught person, it's no wonder we are not hearing more from standers themselves.

Be receptive and compassionate to people who may be fighting a battle behind the scenes to keep a marriage intact or who are on their knees trying to restore a broken relationship. If they are in this posture, you can be very sure they are open to prayer, encouragement, discipleship, and resources to educate them on the possibilities and power they have available to them to fight for a victory. Certainly, it can be a tricky issue dealing with human relationships, but we must always be ready to support them however we can. They are waging a war that has eternal implications.

As God continues to form me into the prodigal Father's likeness, my journey has broadened in scope. I am further up the mountainside and can see more—more of what I have recently traveled through and more of the possibilities that a trusting relationship with God can bring me.

Though I doubt I will hear a ringing affirmation of "Well done!" from anyone else, in my heart and mind I sense God's great pleasure. This journey is for an audience of one. Even if I am on an entirely wrong path, I know that God is very pleased when I try to live out my faithfulness for Him.

For that reason, I wait expectantly to see what God is going to do next in my life. The life interruptions that have visited me recently have seemed more like earthquakes, but I know that He is the God who brings order from chaos. Interruptions like this can be good. They can shake loose some hardened stuff that comes from just living life. I marvel that He loves me enough to do this for me.

Through His grace He is making new wine, birthing a new spirit and filling a new body, a new wineskin, as I die to my old self.

Yet, this is not all I can rejoice in. God promised to repay us for the years the locusts have eaten. My promised one and I will get new life going forward *and* repayment for all that has been lost!

> *I will repay you for the years the locusts have eaten—the great locust and the young locust, the other locusts and the locust swarm—my great army that I sent among you.*
> *You will have plenty to eat, until you are full, and you will praise the name of the Lord your God, who has worked wonders for you; never again will my people be shamed.*
>
> Joel 2:25–26

These verses provide me a great deal of comfort, coming as they do from a God who has the desire and the capacity to make things whole again!

> Do the right thing while you are in God's waiting room.
> Do it because you love Him and because you appreciate all He has done for you.

I continue to practice waiting on God and not allowing myself to run ahead of my own capabilities, staying disciplined in my journey while learning the Lord's lessons where I am.

God had led me far into the wilderness to hear and see and taste the things of Him.

He has led me too far for me to not believe in His great and relentless love for me. He is desiring and contending to bring my prodigal home, so I can throw my arms around her (after those in the presence of the angels get their rejoicing in first! (Luke 15:10)).

My firm belief is that it takes two people giving up to end a marriage. Count me out.

I have faith that, wherever God leads, He provides.

What God initiates, He completes.

His part is provision; my part is trust.

> *"Not by might nor by power, but by my Spirit,"* says the LORD *Almighty.*
>
> Zechariah 4:6

With God's help, I have set my face like flint, knowing that, if it's not good, God's not done.

I've come to experience Him and know I will not be put to shame.

I will not be double-minded, but steadfast.

I will not be denied.
I will not settle.
I will not negotiate.
I will not let go until God blesses me!

I have a vision for restoration. I stoke it and feed it, thereby putting the onus on God.

I know He wants to exercise His power in His house!

When God brought the plagues on Egypt through Moses, Pharaoh finally relented and gave the Israelites *all* they had asked for; so, the Israelites plundered the Egyptians (Exodus 12:36). Not a hoof was to be left behind (Exodus 10:26), and the Egyptians they saw then they would never see again (Exodus 14:13)!

His Word is His final answer.

God's will is not to just heal us but to make us whole, so that we will leave nothing behind or move forward while we are still in need.

This is a rather phenomenal season in my life. I do see things a bit more clearly now, and I am wholly grateful for the Lord's compassion and intimacy. Certainly, my hope is for God's *ruach*, His healing breath to soon rest upon our lives and marriage, yet in some respects I don't want this season of dependance to come to an end. When it does, I am confident that my next season will be one of building on this one—going from strength to strength.

I will continue the battle by following God's path to an ultimate victory of His power and love. In my wait, I will enjoy the rich blessings of Him who has promised that goodness and mercy will follow me all the days of my life.

That is my very imperfect journey thus far.

> *Steadfast love and truth and faithfulness meet together;*
> *Righteousness and peace kiss each other.*
>
> Psalm 85:10 (AMP)

Acknowledgments

I want to give appreciation and praise to God for whispering into my heart, "Write down your journey!" and leading me each step of the way.

While my journey has been about God's revealing new and higher places for me, I have been fortunate to have a pastor who leads with a transparent and searching heart. I have borrowed more of his fought-for wisdom than I care to admit. Thank you, Pastor Randy Harvey of The Crossing Church in The Woodlands, Texas, for encouraging me to pursue God's heart.

Pastor Randy also has a staff who lead with integrity and passion for all things Jesus. Thank you to these pastors who have invested their calling into my life: Pastors Stacy, Reggie, Dr. Lenny, Dale, Christine, Austin, and Allison.

Thank you, too, to Becky Hefty for guidance, mentoring, and encouragement, and to Sharon Bridges for her help with editing.

www.ingramcontent.com/pod-product-compliance
Lightning Source LLC
LaVergne TN
LVHW051524070426
835507LV00023B/3287